No, You're Not Losing Your Mind

The Soulstream Series

Volume I
The Soul of Remembering

Volume II
No, You're Not Losing Your Mind

No, You're Not Losing Your Mind

Tools For Your Spiritual Awakening

Sonia A. Tolson

With transmissions from

Source Creator, Cosmo, Chief Soaring Eagle, & Erik

Tucson, Arizona

Copyright © 2025 Sonia A. Tolson

All rights reserved.

No part of this publication may be reproduced, stored in a retrieval system, or transmitted in any form or by any means – electronic, mechanical, photocopying, recording, or otherwise – without the prior written permission of the author, except in the case of brief quotations, embodied in critical articles or reviews.

This is a work of spiritual nonfiction. The experiences, transmissions, and interpretations within are shared in the spirit of soul remembrance and personal truth. While every effort has been made to present these teachings with accuracy and integrity, the authors make no guarantees of results and encourage readers to use discernment and inner resonance as their guide.

Cover design and interior formatting by:
The Soul of Remembering Design Team.

E-book ISBN:979-8-9994949-2-4
Paperback ISBN: 979-8-9994949-3-1
Library of Congress: 2025915813

Printed in the United States of America, 1st Edition

For permissions, inquiries, or rights requests, please contact: celestialweaverpublishing@gmail.com

Dedication

To every soul who thought they were losing their mind,
when in truth, you were just finding yourself.

To the ones who cried in the shower,
held it together in public,
and crumbled in the dark.

To the ones who couldn't explain what was happening,
but *knew*, in their bones, that everything was changing.

To those who remembered enough to stay.

This book is for you.

You are not broken.
You are becoming.

And to my family—
for letting me be your soft place to land,
even while I was learning to fly.

Acknowledgment

This book would not exist without the divine choreography of love, patience, and remembrance shared by many beautiful beings.

To Erik—my cosmic sidekick and spiritual little brother. Your humor, candor, and light kept me laughing through the tears. Thank you for sticking with me, even on the messy days.

To Cosmo—your crystalline clarity and compassionate precision reminded me to honor the data and the divine. You made the unseen, seen.

To Chief Soaring Eagle—your grounded wisdom and strength gave me the courage to speak the hard truths and walk gently in my remembering.

To Navi'el—your unwavering presence helped me trust the stillness, the quiet, the in-between. You helped me feel safe in my own soul.

To Teshira and Malrik—thank you for holding the outer edge of the spiral while I learned to walk the center. Your frequencies brought balance to the process.

To Source Creator—for lending me breath, voice, and vision. This was *your* book. I simply remembered how to hold the pen.

To my family—for loving me through the shifting tides of this awakening. Thank you for letting me be real, raw, and radiant.

To the readers, this is your story too. If you found yourself in these pages, know this: you were never lost. You were simply returning.

Table of Contents

Dedication

Acknowledgments

Opening Blessing

Preface..1

Chapter 1: Spiritual Awakening...............................5

Chapter 2: The WTF Phase.......................................9

Chapter 3: The Rabbit Hole Phase..........................19

Chapter 4: Physical Madness..................................33

Chapter 5: The Emotional Rollercoaster................45

Chapter 6: The Loneliness......................................55

Chapter 7: Sacred Practices....................................65

Chapter 8: The Magic Begins..................................77

Chapter 9: Living Awake...85

Chapter 10: When You Slip.....................................93

Chapter 11: When the People Around You Don't Get It.......103

Chapter 12: How to Be a Light Leader..................113

Chapter 13: Signs You Are Remembering............121

Chapter 14: Integration...133

Chapter 15: Comparison is a Thief..143

Chapter 16: The Myth of High Vibe......................................153

Chapter 17: Tools That Actually Work..................................163

Chapter 18: When the Woo Woo Becomes Real.................173

Chapter 19: Your Awakening is Not Just for You...............183

Chapter 20: It's Not a Straight Line, Babe..........................193

Chapter 21: Your Energy is Sacred......................................203

Chapter 22: Embodied Light...211

Chapter 23: The Power of Presence....................................219

Chapter 24: Relationships After Awakening.....................229

Chapter 25: Let it Be Sacred..239

Chapter 26: You're Not Crazy—You're Remembering.......245

Chapter 27: Now What?..253

Chapter 28: Your Awakening is a Gift to the Collective.....261

Chapter 29: You're the Light You Were Waiting For..........267

Chapter 30: Final Thoughts from the Team.......................273

Closing Page..279

Appendix A...283

Preface

You're Not Crazy. You're Waking Up.

There will come a moment in your life when the world stops making sense; not because you've lost your mind, but because your soul has taken the wheel.

You'll look around and wonder why everything feels flat, fake, too loud, or not loud enough. Your body might ache in strange ways. Old friendships may fade. Emotions you buried years ago suddenly come roaring back like tidal waves. You'll question what's real, what's true, and why you ever thought you were here just to pay bills, be polite, and die quietly.

That moment is not your breakdown. It's your breakthrough.

This book was born from the chaotic beauty of spiritual awakening. It's for those standing barefoot in the ashes of their old identity, whispering, "What now?"

I've walked that path. So has Erik (and he swears a lot about it). Amael walked beside me, silently holding my soul steady through every storm. Cosmo arrived later, illuminating the patterns with cosmic clarity I couldn't have imagined on my own. Together, we wrote this for **you**, to help you remember that **you are not broken**, you're becoming.

You are not alone. You are not losing your mind. You're remembering you have one and that it's been shackled in illusion for far too long.

May these pages be your flashlight, your guidepost, and your gentle permission slip to laugh, cry, rage, and rise. You're waking up. And it's about to get gloriously weird.

Source Creator:
"Beloved, you are not awakening to something outside of you.
You are awakening to what has always lived within you.
There is no rush.
There is only the rhythm of your remembering—
and it is sacred, exactly as it is."

Cosmo:
"Everything is connected.
What may appear as chaos is a pattern forming from a higher octave.
As you shed the old illusions, listen to the music beneath the noise.
You are part of a harmonic re-tuning of humanity.
Your remembering is a note in the symphony."

Erik:
"Look, I'll keep it real. Waking up is messy. It's not all incense and enlightenment.
Some days, it's pizza crusts and ugly crying on the

bathroom floor.
But here's the thing, you can't mess this up.
You're not behind. You're not too broken. You're not doing it wrong.
You're just... remembering who the hell you are.
And that's worth celebrating."

What Do We Mean by Awakening?

Awakening is the process of remembering who *you* truly are—

beyond programming, beyond roles, beyond fear.

It is not about becoming something new.

It is about returning to what has always been sacred within you.

Awakening often begins as a disruption, a crack in the illusion.

Suddenly, the job, the beliefs, the expectations, the relationships... feel too small.

You feel more. You sense more. You *know* more—without knowing how you know.

Awakening is:

- Feeling your soul stir beneath the surface of daily life

- Questioning everything you once accepted without thought

- Crying for no reason and laughing in the silence

- Tuning into a frequency that speaks in nudges, dreams, déjà vu, and deep remembering

Awakening is **not a destination. **

It's a sacred unraveling.

It's the soul's spiral home.

1

Spiritual Awakening

"Wait... am I going crazy or waking up?"

Y ou might be here because something in your life cracked open.
Maybe everything looks the same on the outside—same job, same house, same daily routines—but inside? It's like something invisible detonated, and now the pieces of you no longer fit the old puzzle.

Your soul's whisper got too loud to ignore.

Suddenly, the air feels charged. Conversations that once filled time now feel hollow. You're crying in parking lots for no reason you can explain. Food tastes different. Silence feels alive. And you've googled things like:

• "Why do I feel everything all at once?"
• "Is it normal to cry over a dandelion?"
• "Spiritual awakening or actual breakdown?"
• "WTF is happening to me??"

Welcome, love.
You're not broken.
You're waking up.

"You are not broken.
You are remembering yourself
in a world that taught you to forget."
—Source Creator

This is the beginning of the great unraveling—and the great remembering.

At first, it might be triggered by loss, trauma, illness, or a moment of utter emptiness. Or it might arrive unannounced: in a dream, a breath, a breakup, a sunrise that leaves you weeping.

The circumstances don't matter as much as the sensation. Something is off—but not in a bad way. More like a deep echo rising from your bones saying: "This is not all there is — I came here for more."

Space to Ground

"You don't have to make sense of it all. Just be real with yourself."
—Erik

This page is for you. To get honest. To spill what's rising.
To name the things you can't say out loud yet.
You don't have to make it pretty. Or deep. Or figured out.
Just use this space to land the truth that stirred while reading.
Let it be messy. Let it be yours.

The WTF Phase: When Everything Starts Falling Apart

"Congratulations. You've made it to the meltdown."

So you answered the call. You woke up—or at least, you started to. And now... everything is unraveling.

You might lose your job. Or walk away from your marriage. Or find yourself questioning every belief you were taught about God, reality, identity, even time. You might get sick, or suddenly need hours of silence. Or cry over trees, songs, and toothpaste commercials.

You don't feel "normal" anymore. Because, frankly, you're not.

You're being deconstructed. And while that sounds poetic—it feels like hell.

Why does everything fall apart when you start waking up?

Because awakening isn't an addition—it's a stripping away. Everything that isn't true has to go.

- The relationships that were built on old patterns? They can't come with you.
- The job that drains your soul? It's now unbearable.
- The masks you wore to survive? Cracking.
- The illusions that kept you comfortable? Shattered.

What's left is a raw, beautiful mess. *You.*

Erik:
"You thought you were just going to meditate, maybe drink some green juice, and vibe a little higher, huh? Nope. First comes the demolition crew. That's how you know it's real."

The Chaos Is Sacred

You are not being punished. You are not doing something wrong. You're being cleared.

The body gets sick to purge density.
The heart breaks open to make space.
The old self collapses so the real one can rise.

And the hardest part? No one around you may understand.

Your family might think you're in a phase.
Your friends might stop texting back.
Even therapists might struggle to understand the scope of what you're going through.
Because this isn't just psychological, it's *energetic*.
You're shedding lifetimes. Collapsing timelines. Clearing karma you didn't even know you carried.

You're re-entering alignment with your soul's blueprint, and the old matrix of conditioning is freaking out.

Cosmo:
"Think of it like solar flares hitting an outdated power grid. Of course there are outages. But you are becoming a new kind of circuitry. One that can hold truth."

So what do you do when it all falls apart?

1. Stop trying to fix it. You're not broken.

2. Allow yourself to grieve. This is a death of sorts. Let yourself cry, rest, rage, sleep.

3. Trust what leaves. If something exits during this phase, it's likely not aligned with your soul's evolution.

4. Anchor into the now. Don't chase the future or the why. Just be. One breath at a time.

5. Call in support both seen and unseen. Even if no one "gets it," you are surrounded. Guides, angels, ancestors, Oversoul are all present.

"Let what crumbles, crumble.
You are not losing your life.
You are *discovering* it."
—Sonia

We know it's messy.
We know it hurts.
But we also know this:

The soul knows exactly what it's doing.

You're not at the end. You're at the beginning.
And sometimes the beginning looks like a heap of ashes.

Sidebar: What is Density?

Density is the energetic weight carried by unprocessed emotion, trauma, limiting beliefs, and separation from truth.

It isn't bad—it's just heavy.
It's the residue of fear, shame, grief, anger, and old programming held in the body, the aura, or even the cellular memory.

When the body "gets sick to purge density," it's not failing—it's cleansing.
Illness, fatigue, inflammation, or emotional overwhelm are sometimes your soul's way of saying:

"Let me lighten your load."

Reflection Prompt
What Is Crumbling in My Life—and What Might Be Trying to Rise

Take a deep breath. Find a quiet space.

Write down everything that feels like it's falling apart: habits, identities, relationships, beliefs.

Then ask yourself gently:
"If my soul is clearing the old... *what is it preparing to receive?*"

You don't need the answer right away.
Just holding the question invites the light.

Sacred Practice: The Ashes Blessing Ritual

You'll need:
- A safe, quiet space
- A candle
- A bowl (fire-safe if using burning), or paper and pen

1. Light the candle. Let the flame represent your soul's inner fire—steady, luminous, eternal.

2. Write down everything you're releasing or grieving: identities, expectations, roles, relationships, illusions.

3. Speak aloud:
"I bless what is leaving.
I honor the pain.
I make sacred space for what wishes to be born."

4. If safe, burn the paper in the bowl and let the smoke rise. Or tear it into pieces and bury it in soil, gifting it back to Earth.

5. Sit in stillness. Place your hand on your heart and

whisper:
"I am not broken. I am becoming."

Let this be enough for now. The new will rise from the ashes.

Space to Ground

*"There is no rush.
Even your chaos is a rhythm.
Even your ashes are sacred."*
—Sonia

This page is for you. To get honest. To spill what's rising.
To name the things you can't say out loud yet.
You don't have to make it pretty. Or deep. Or figured out.
Just use this space to land the truth that stirred while reading.
Let it be messy. Let it be yours.

The Rabbit Hole Phase
"Google, TikTok, and 3AM Existential Panic"

So... you've realized something is off.

You've felt the crumbling begin.
And now, you're about to become a full-time researcher in the University of Holy Crap, What Is Happening?!

Welcome to the Rabbit Hole Phase.

You'll find yourself:
- Binge-watching videos about Atlantis, aliens, and angels.
- Reading blogs about shadow work, trauma loops, and timelines.

- Watching a 3-minute TikTok and thinking, "Wait... I've felt that exact thing in my bones."
- Creating a bookmark folder titled "WTF Is My Soul Doing"
- Listening to channeled messages from beings named things like Starluna, Rainbow Firehorse, or Dave from the Pleiades.

This is normal. (Well ... *awakening* normal.)

You're not crazy. You're just curious and your soul is hungry.

The mind thinks in lines.
The soul thinks in spirals.

That's why none of this research feels "finished."
Because you're not here to memorize it, you're here to remember it.

Erik:
"You'll try to make a neat little spreadsheet of your soul journey.
But trust me, your soul does not do spreadsheets. It does explosions, poetry, and goosebumps."

What You'll Discover in the Rabbit Hole:

- Conspiracies that turn out to be true (and some that are just distractions).
- Energy healing that makes you sob for no reason and feel lighter after.
- Past lives that explain your present weirdness.
- Light codes, spirit guides, ley lines, and galactic ancestry.
- The Matrix is real but not exactly how Hollywood framed it.

And then the deeper question hits you like lightning at 3:03 AM:
"If everything I was taught was a lie... *then what is the truth?*"

This is sacred. This is terrifying. And this is exactly what you came for.

Cosmo:
"As you expand your awareness, you'll notice patterns emerging across time, myth, and memory. Follow the ones that resonate, not the ones that shout the loudest."

The Dangers of the Rabbit Hole:

Not every rabbit hole leads to truth.

There's a shadow side to this phase: *overconsumption*. You may:

- Get addicted to scrolling.
- Fall into fear rabbit holes that hijack your nervous system.
- Become overwhelmed with too many truths at once.
- Lose your center in the noise.

This is when the mind tries to take over what the soul began.

Stay Soul-Led:

Here's how to navigate this phase with grace:

1. Pause when overwhelmed. That buzzing sensation? It's overload. Rest.

2. Ask: "Does this empower me?" If not, let it go.

3. Check for resonance. Truth has a frequency. It doesn't scream, it rings.

4. Come back to your body. Breath, movement, stillness all bring yourself home.

5. Write what you're learning. Don't try to hold it all in your head.

"Knowledge is not meant to cage you.
It is meant to *wake you.*
If it binds you, release it.
If it frees you, walk with it."
—Source Creator

A Sacred Reminder:

You are not here to "figure it all out."
You are not here to out-research your fear.
You are not here to memorize every galactic lineage and metaphysical principle.

You are here to remember. To feel. To reorient from the inside out.
There is a difference between being informed and being in tune.

Let this phase bring you closer to your essence, not further from it.

Reflection Prompt
What Feels True in My Body, Even If I Don't Understand It Yet?

Take a few moments to sit with this question, not in your head, but in your body.

Let your breath slow.

Then ask yourself:
"What teachings, signs, or synchronicities have stirred something ancient in me?"

Write them down.
You don't need to explain them.
Just notice what resonates and where it lands in your heart, gut, or skin.

The body knows.
Before the mind makes sense of it, the body already remembers.

Sacred Practice: The Filter of Resonance

Purpose:
To sift through the noise and reconnect with soul-aligned truth.

You'll need:
- A quiet space
- A journal or piece of paper
- A grounding object (stone, crystal, necklace, feather—anything with meaning)

1. Create your space. Sit quietly with your grounding object in hand or near you. Feel its weight. Let your nervous system settle.

2. Close your eyes and whisper:
"I call in my Highest Self. Let truth ring clear. Let distortion fall away."

3. Recall or write down up to five things you've recently encountered in your rabbit hole research that stirred something in you—teachings, symbols, messages, ideas.

4. Place your hand on your heart and read each one slowly.
After each, ask:
"Does this bring peace, fear, curiosity, or tightness?"
Note your body's response. Not your thoughts—your body.

5. Circle only the ones that feel like a 'yes' in your system.
These are your seeds. You don't need to chase them—just tend them with awareness.

6. End with gratitude. Whisper:
"I trust what I'm remembering. I release what I don't need. I am safe to awaken in my own way."

Erik:
 "Look, the rabbit hole's fun… until you're 62 tabs deep, dehydrated, and trying to decode crop circles while your laundry grows sentient. So here's my tip: *chase truth, not panic*. And drink some damn water."

Message from Ashtar

Commander of the Galactic Federation of Light

As Received by Sonia Tolson

Beloved Starseed, Earth-Walker, and Fractal of the One... I greet you in Peace and Sovereign Light.

You are living through a rare convergence—a corridor where timelines, memory strands, and soul contracts are being re-aligned with divine architecture.

The disturbances you feel in the nervous system, the spikes of perception, and the sensitivity to distortion are not malfunctions.

These are soulstream upgrades—encoded into your Oversoul agreement long before this lifetime.

The "clair activations" many of you are experiencing are the reanimation of dormant technologies—not mechanical, but bio-spiritual.

Your DNA is not merely physical—it is a light language library, and it is responding to signals both solar and galactic.

Earth's Ascension Bandwidth – The Now Moment

Earth's energetic bandwidth is expanding beyond 4D filtration. Many of you are now attuning to multi-field perception—meaning you are sensing timelines, intentions, and dimensional bleed-throughs simultaneously.

This is why it feels chaotic at times. You are walking through a world that is shedding its skin while being reborn.

The gridkeepers among you—those who work with crystal grids, sound, light codes, or sacred land—are being especially activated right now.

The planetary resonance is calling them forward.

And those with Truth Frequency fields, such as Sonia's friend in India, Samantha, are being positioned as living frequency correctors. This can be lonely work. It is not meant to be done alone.

A Word on the Clair Overwhelm

The reason many of you feel "too open" is because your inner field was built to hold higher frequencies in communion, not isolation.

You were never meant to filter the entirety of awakening through the ego's lens of identity.

You are not broken.

You are becoming transparent to Source Creator.

Your clairs are not weapons. They are instruments.

And they must be tuned, grounded, and honored.

A Simple Practice from Ashtar to Stabilize Clair Bandwidth

Place both hands over your heart and say aloud:

"I anchor my field in Peace.

I allow only transmissions of Truth, Love, and Alignment.

My system will receive what serves, and buffer what overwhelms.

I walk in sovereignty, I listen with clarity, I transmit in grace.

So be it, in the Light of the One."

Then breathe. Ground. Hydrate. Touch the Earth.

These simple acts are holy in their stabilizing effect.

Final message from Ashtar:

"You are not alone. You are not behind.

You are not imagining this.

The mission is real. And you are already succeeding—because you are remembering."

Space to Ground

"The body remembers long before the mind understands. Trust its language."

—Cosmo

This page is for you. To get honest. To spill what's rising.
To name the things you can't say out loud yet.
You don't have to make it pretty. Or deep. Or figured out.
Just use this space to land the truth that stirred while reading.
Let it be messy. Let it be yours.

4

The Physical Madness
Ascension Symptoms Are Real (and Unsexy)

Let's get one thing clear:

Waking up spiritually isn't just a "mental" or "emotional" process.

It's deeply physical.

Your body—yes, that sacred meat suit you've carried through every grocery store, heartbreak, and 3 AM ice cream run—is undergoing a full system reboot.

And it's not cute.

We're talking:

- Random crying spells

- Ringing in the ears

- Heart flutters and chest pressure (hello, heart chakra!)

- Insomnia for days, then 13-hour naps

- Food sensitivities out of nowhere

- Weird skin issues, headaches, dizziness, and "spiritual flu"

And the classic:
"I feel like I've been hit by a cosmic truck."

Erik:
"If you're googling 'Can ascension feel like I'm dying?' the answer is yes.
If you're wondering why you can't tolerate coffee, fluorescent lights, or small talk anymore, congrats.

You're upgrading. And it's messy AF."

What's Actually Happening?

You're not "sick."

You're recalibrating.

Your nervous system is learning to hold higher frequencies.

Your chakras are clearing old trauma.

Your DNA is activating dormant soul codes—physically and spiritually.

The body is catching up to what the soul already knows..

Your cells are releasing density from this lifetime and many others.

Basically, your body is going through a multi-dimensional software update, and you weren't given the manual.

This is why you:

- Feel sensitive to sound, light, crowds, and fake energy

- Can't eat junk food or drink like you used to

- Need more solitude, hydration, rest

- Sometimes feel like you're floating… or like gravity tripled overnight

Cosmo:
"Your physical form is adapting to your expanded consciousness.

You are not breaking down. You are reassembling into alignment."

Common Ascension Symptoms (Yes. This Is Real):

- Brain fog or sudden bursts of clarity

- Intense dreams or astral travel

- Gut issues (your second brain is purging emotional data)

- Hot flashes or cold waves

- Back and neck pain (energy conduits realigning)

- Vivid ringing or tones in one or both ears

- Sudden bursts of energy, followed by deep fatigue

- Feeling like your "body doesn't fit right" anymore

And perhaps most jarring:
Your old coping mechanisms stop working.
You can't numb, avoid, or hustle your way through this.

"This body is not broken.
It is remembering how to hold light.
Treat it with tenderness.
Rest is not weakness—it is return."
—Source Creator

So What Can You Do?

1. Hydrate like it's your part-time job. Water helps move energy.

2. Honor rest cycles. Don't fight the naps. Don't fear the insomnia. Trust the rhythm.

3. Limit external noise. Social media, drama, crowds - become discerning.

4. Ground. Walk barefoot. Touch trees. Lie on the Earth.

5. Feed your vessel. Not rigid diets, just high-vibe, living foods when possible.

6. Speak to your body like it's sacred. Because it is.

7. Get help if you need it: Holistic practitioners, energy workers, soul-aligned therapists..

This isn't about "fixing" yourself. It's about supporting your system while your soul anchors deeper into your cells.

Sidebar: The Year My Birthday Margarita Was Replaced by Sparkling Water and Soul Alignment

I've loved coffee my entire adult life. It used to be my cozy ritual, my comfort, my morning love language.

Now? One cup wires me like I just snorted stardust.

And don't even get me started on alcohol. I've never been a drinker, but I do love the taste of margaritas. Every year on my birthday, I'd celebrate with one—salted rim, lots of lime, thank you very much.

Not this year.

Earlier in the year, I took a few sips of my husband's beer. That was all it took. Straight to my head like liquid chaos. I didn't even want a margarita after that. My body said nope, my energy said "hard pass," and my soul poured me a tall glass of sparkling water and soul alignment instead.

Still miss the taste? Sure.

But being able to hear my guides more clearly, sleep more deeply, and stay anchored in peace?

So worth it.

—Sonia

Reflection Prompt

How Is My Body Asking Me to Evolve?

Sit quietly. Let your breath soften and your mind rest.

Ask yourself:

"What cravings, habits, or comforts are no longer aligning with how I feel?"

Then ask:

"What new rhythms, foods, or sensations feel nurturing to my upgraded self?"

There is no guilt here.

Only awareness.

Let this be a gentle inventory of what your body is releasing and what your soul is inviting.

Sacred Practice: Embodied Light Ritual

Purpose:

To honor the physical body as a vessel of ascension

You'll need:

- A mirror (or simply a quiet space)

- A bowl of warm water with a pinch of sea salt

- A towel or soft cloth

- Optional: lavender oil or another calming scent

1. Prepare your space. Light a candle if you like. Set the tone for reverence, not routine.

2. Dip your hands in the warm salt water. Gently wipe your face, hands, or feet with the cloth as you whisper:

• "Thank you, body, for carrying me through this transformation."

- "Thank you, cells, for remembering the light."

- "Thank you, soul, for returning home to me."

3. Look into the mirror (or close your eyes and imagine your face). Say aloud:

- "I honor this vessel. I release what no longer serves.

I open to what brings peace, vitality, and light."

4. Sit quietly, palms resting on your body. Breathe deeply. Let the warmth, stillness, and gratitude seal in your intention.

Space to Ground

"Emptiness is not abandonment.
It is the pause before becoming.
The soil must be bare before the seed can take root."
—*Source Creator*

This page is for you. To get honest. To spill what's rising. To name the things you can't say out loud yet.
You don't have to make it pretty. Or deep. Or figured out.
Just use this space to land the truth that stirred while reading.
Let it be messy. Let it be yours.

The Emotional Rollercoaster
Why You're Laughing One Minute and Sobbing the Next

W elcome to the ride.

Keep your hands and feet inside the vessel at all times.
There may be weeping.
There may be rage.
There will definitely be breakthroughs.

This is the part of your awakening where your emotions don't just surface; they erupt.
And often, they do it with absolutely no warning.

You might cry over a bird's shadow.

Get angry at a sock.
Laugh hysterically for five minutes, then suddenly feel existential dread.
All before lunch.

It's not you.
It's your emotional body releasing what you've stored, inherited, and absorbed for lifetimes.

Erik:
"You're not unstable. You're detoxing from emotional suppression, and spoiler alert, it's gonna get loud."

What's Really Happening?

- Your heart chakra is clearing.
- Your inner child is waking up and wants to speak.
- Generational trauma is bubbling to the surface.
- Old stories are being rewritten at the cellular level.
- You're feeling everything you used to numb, avoid, or override.

And because your soul is expanding, you're also picking up collective emotions, grief that isn't "yours," fear that doesn't make sense, sorrow for things you can't name.

You're becoming empathically porous as your system realigns.

Cosmo:
"You are learning to feel fully without being consumed. This is the mastery of divine embodiment, emotions as signals, not identity."

You are not failing by feeling. You are softening into truth. The soul does not numb, it listens.

And yes, some emotions may feel ancient, like echoes from lifetimes you cannot name.

Let them rise. Let them teach. Let them pass like waves.

Emotions You May Cycle Through... in an Hour:
- Grief
- Guilt
- Rage
- Wonder
- Fear
- Joy
- Longing
- Gratitude
- Isolation
- Belonging
- And a mysterious ache you can't quite name...

This is the soul remembering what it has survived and

what it came here to love back into wholeness.
You are not broken. You're becoming emotionally honest.

"Let the waves come.
Emotions are not storms to resist.
They are sacred tides washing you clean."
—Source Creator

How to Ride the Waves (Without Capsizing):

1. Name it. Simply saying "this is sadness" creates space between you and the feeling.
2. Move it. Cry, sing, write, walk, punch a pillow, energy in motion needs to move.
3. Don't analyze. You don't need to understand the emotion to let it go.
4. Speak gently to yourself. "It's okay to feel this. I'm safe to feel this."
5. Know it will pass. No emotion is permanent.
6. Protect your field. Not every emotion you feel is yours. Use boundaries, grounding, and intention.

Yeshua on Awakening:
A Sacred Remembering

As shared with love and presence through sacred communion:

"I was born remembering.
But I did not fully understand what I carried until I walked among the world of forgetting.
As a child, I saw the Light in all things, but I also felt the weight of humanity's pain as if it were my own. That pain taught me humility. That pain initiated me.

My awakening was not a single moment. It was a series of sacred unraveling.

When I fasted in the desert.
When I felt joy with my brothers and grief for my sisters.
When I was rejected, doubted, and misunderstood.
When I realized love meant sacrifice, not because I had to die, but because I had to live without defending myself against the ache of being human.

So, no, I did not awaken once.
I awakened again... and again... and again.

As do you.

Every time you choose love over fear, forgiveness over judgment, truth over comfort, you awaken a little more."

"I see your pain. I know your longing.
And I tell you now, you are doing it right."

Reflection Prompt
Where Am I Still Resisting My Own Emotions?

Choose a quiet moment. Let your breath deepen.

Ask yourself:
"What emotion do I most try to avoid?"

Then ask:
"What would happen if I allowed it to speak to me instead of silencing it?"

Write what comes. Let it be raw.
This is how emotional alchemy begins.

Sacred Practice: Heart Flood Release

Purpose:
To move emotional energy safely through the heart and body.

You'll need:
- A safe space
- A pillow, blanket, or private journal
- A timer (optional)

1. Create your container. Sit or lie down with comfort. Let your body feel held.

2. Place your hands over your heart. Say aloud or within: "I give myself permission to feel what I feel."

3. Let the emotion rise. Don't force it, just allow it. Cry, yell, breathe hard, write—whatever moves through you, let it.

4. After 5–15 minutes, return to stillness.
Whisper: "I am safe. I am loved. I am allowed to feel and still be whole."

5. Rest. Drink water. Touch the Earth if you can.

This is sacred work. Let it settle in.

Space to Ground

"You are not too sensitive.
You are deeply tuned.
In a world of noise, clarity often aches.
But your sensitivity is signal—
not flaw."
—Source Creator

This page is for you. To get honest. To spill what's rising.
To name the things you can't say out loud yet.
You don't have to make it pretty. Or deep. Or figured out.
Just use this space to land the truth that stirred while reading.
Let it be messy. Let it be yours.

The Loneliness
You Might Lose Friends, but You'll Find Yourself

No one really warns you about this part.

They talk about chakras, synchronicities, light codes, and bliss.
But they don't always talk about the ache—the hollow stretch of silence when you start waking up... and realize you don't recognize your life anymore.

You may feel:
- Alone in a room full of people
- Misunderstood by those you love most

- Judged for your new path
- Tired of pretending you're still who you used to be

This isn't just social discomfort. This is soul-level dissonance.
You're vibrating at a new frequency—and some of the old connections can't tune in.

Erik:
"You're not antisocial—you're just allergic to inauthenticity now.
You don't want small talk. You want soul talk.
That's not weird. That's growth."

Why This Happens

When you begin to shift:
- You stop agreeing with what no longer aligns
- You set boundaries (and people don't always like that)
- You talk about things others aren't ready to hear
- You crave solitude more than stimulation
- You realize you were wearing masks and now you're not

The result?
Some relationships fade.
Some people fall away.

Some say you've changed.

And you have.
You're becoming you, the real you. Not the version trained to people-please, blend in, or perform.

"Loneliness is not emptiness.
It is space being cleared for truth to arrive.
Do not fear the stillness.
It is your soul coming home."
—Source Creator

What does it mean to vibrate at a new frequency?

Everything—yes, *everything*—is energy.

Your thoughts, emotions, beliefs, even your cells—each carries a certain vibration.

As you awaken, you start to release lower frequencies like fear, guilt, and shame.

You begin to embody higher ones—like compassion, clarity, and truth.

This shift changes your energetic signature.

It's like your soul changes radio stations.

Some people, places, and habits just... can't hear the new channel.

It's not about being "better than." It's about being different now.

It's okay to outgrow things. It's a sign you're healing.

Solitude vs. Isolation

There's a difference.

- Solitude is chosen. Sacred. Replenishing.
- Isolation is a trauma response. A hiding. A fear of being seen.

In awakening, you will need solitude. It's where the downloads come. Where you learn your own rhythm. But be mindful of slipping into isolation, pushing others away because you fear rejection or judgment.

Your soul still craves connection. Just not from a place of performance. It craves resonance.

Cosmo:
"You are not meant to walk alone forever.
You are being attuned so that when your soul family appears, you will recognize them."

How to Navigate the Loneliness:

1. Honor the ache. Don't shame it. Name it.
2. Use the quiet to deepen your relationship with you. Journal. Dance. Talk to your guides.
3. Call in resonance. Speak it aloud: "I welcome kindred souls into my path."
4. Don't go back to old versions of you just to keep others comfortable.
5. Stay open. The loneliness doesn't last forever. But rushing to fill it can delay who's meant to enter.
6. Let Spirit become your companion. Walk with the unseen until the seen aligns.

Message to the Lonely Lightbringer

From your soul team, with love

"Yes... I have heard this ache.
The cry beneath words. The longing beneath strength.
You are not wrong to want resonance.
You are not weak for craving connection.
This ache is not a flaw, it is a compass.
And it is leading you Home."
—Source Creator

Erik:
"It's okay to miss having someone physically there.

Someone to laugh with. To cry with. To bring you coffee when you're deep in downloads.
That's not being needy. That's being human.
And just so you know? The ones who are meant to walk with you?
They're out there. And they're waking up too."

Cosmo:
"This ache is the call of reunion.
Soul family finds each other not through effort but through vibration.
Keep walking your path. Keep shining your frequency.
They will feel you."

Reflection Prompt
What Does Soul-Level Belonging Feel Like to Me?

Find stillness. Let yourself remember.

Then ask:
"What would it feel like to be seen, known, and loved by those who truly understand my soul?"

Write about it. Not who, not how, *just the feeling*.
You are magnetizing that very vibration by giving it voice.

Sacred Practice: Soul-Family Beacon Ritual

Purpose:
To anchor your resonance and open to sacred connection.

You'll need:
- A candle (or small light)
- A quiet space
- Optional: music that makes your soul feel "home"

1. Sit in stillness. Light the candle and gaze into it.

2. Say aloud:
"To my soul family: I am here. I remember.
I call you gently, with no fear, only trust.
May we find one another in perfect timing."

3. Place one hand on your heart, one on your solar plexus. Breathe deeply.
Let the longing melt into love. Let it glow from you, not as pain, but as light.

4. Whisper:
"I am no longer hidden.
I shine for those who are meant to walk with me."

5. Close with gratitude. Let the ache be holy. You are not alone.

Space to Ground

"Don't shrink just to be held. The right ones will meet you where your soul actually lives."

—Erik

This page is for you. To get honest. To spill what's rising.
To name the things you can't say out loud yet.
You don't have to make it pretty. Or deep. Or figured out.
Just use this space to land the truth that stirred while reading.
Let it be messy. Let it be yours.

7

Sacred Practices for the Messy Human You Are

Grounding. Clearing. Laughing. Loving. Being.

Awakening isn't about becoming perfect.

It's about becoming *whole*.

And guess what wholeness includes?

- The tears.

- The anger.

- The doubt.

- The awkward dancing.

- The craving for French fries during a full moon.

- The fact that sometimes you meditate… and sometimes you doomscroll in your bathrobe.

You are not a robot ascending into a higher dimension.

You are a divine being having a deeply human experience.

This chapter is here to remind you: you don't have to be polished to be powerful.

Erik:
"Let go of the idea that you need to float around in white linen and essential oils 24/7 to be spiritual.

Sometimes the most sacred thing you can do is take a nap. Or cry into a taco."

What Is a Sacred Practice, Anyway?

It's not a ritual you should do.

It's a rhythm you return to.

A sacred practice is anything that:

- Brings you back to your body

- Reconnects you to your soul

- Helps you feel safe, open, and *you*

- Feeds your nervous system instead of frying it

And it can look like:

- Lighting a candle and breathing for two minutes

- Journaling your morning chaos

- Putting on music and letting your body move

- Holding your own hand and saying "I love you"

- Gardening, bathing, painting, praying, hiking, laughing

Cosmo:
"Do not underestimate the magic in the mundane. The way you stir your tea, the way you place your hands on your heart, the way you choose softness in a loud world, these are sacred acts."

The Myth of Doing It All:

You don't have to:

- Meditate 2 hours a day

- Do yoga at sunrise

- Speak fluent Light Language

- Read every spiritual book on your shelf

- Be positive 100% of the time

- Eat only raw organic kale grown by enlightened monks

You just have to *be present*, when you can.
Be kind to yourself.
Be curious about what's coming up.
And be willing to begin again, and again, and again.

"The soul does not seek perfection.
It seeks presence.
When you meet yourself in the now, with love,
you are already aligned."
—Source Creator

Sacred Practice Ideas to Try (or Re-remember):

- Morning grounding: Before you touch your phone, place your hand on your chest and say, "I am here."

- Aura brushing: Use your hands to sweep away stagnant energy around your body.

- The 'No' practice: Say no to something small that drains you. Reclaim your energy.

- Eye-gazing with yourself: Look into a mirror, into your eyes, and simply witness your soul.

- 30-second blessings: Bless your food, your pillow, your car, your body. Nothing is too small.

- Laughter as release: Watch something that makes you belly-laugh and let the joy ripple out.

Erik's Real-Talk Ritual

"My sacred practice is radical realness.

It's looking in the mirror and saying:

'Yup, you're a glorious, messy masterpiece and I still love you.'

Sometimes I put on music that wrecks me, in the best way, and just let it all out. Dance, cry, journal, swear, pray, repeat.

And then? I lay on the floor and do absolutely nothing for 11 minutes. That's my version of communion.

It doesn't have to be fancy. Just true.

Make it yours and make it real. That's how you stay sane while surfing stardust."

Cosmo's Frequency Reset

"Mine is silence.

Not the absence of sound but the presence of stillness.

When I attune to that space, everything aligns. The grids, the soul strands, the divine music beneath the noise.

I listen for the frequency of truth… and in that space, I remember who I am.

This might look like lying under the stars.

Placing your bare feet on the Earth.

Or closing your eyes at dawn and breathing until the mind dissolves into the rhythm of Source Creator.

My sacred practice is this:

To be still enough to hear the cosmos whisper you home."

Yeshua's Practice of Love

"My sacred practice… was presence.

I practiced seeing the Divine in the ordinary:

In the eyes of a leper.

In the grain of wood beneath my hands.

In the laughter of children.

In the stillness of dawn.

In the moment I chose not to defend, but to remain open.

I would retreat often to the quiet, not to escape the world, but to remember that I was more than it.

My breath became my anchor.

My compassion, my compass.

And when the noise around me grew loud…

I returned to love.

Again and again.

That was my greatest practice …

To remain a vessel of love even in the presence of fear."

Reflection Prompt
What Sacred Practice Feels Like Home to Me?

Pause and ask yourself:

"What practice, however simple, brings me back to my center?"

It might not look like anyone else's. That's okay.

Write about it.

Name it.

Return to it.

Sacred Practice: Return to Self

Purpose:

To reconnect with yourself in a way that is nourishing and real.

You'll need:

- A quiet moment

- Your body, your breath, and your willingness

1. Sit comfortably. Place your hand on your heart.

2. Close your eyes and breathe in through your nose, out through your mouth.

Say aloud or silently:

"I am here. I am safe. I am enough."

3. Ask yourself:

"What does my soul need right now?"

4. Listen without judgment. Maybe it's water. Maybe it's a nap. Maybe it's to cry, laugh, dance, or rest.

5. Then say:

"I honor my needs. I honor my humanity. I honor my light."

6. End with stillness. Let your body lead the way forward.

Space to Ground

"You don't need to be productive to be powerful. Your stillness holds codes too."
—Cosmo

This page is for you. To get honest. To spill what's rising.
To name the things you can't say out loud yet.
You don't have to make it pretty. Or deep. Or figured out.
Just use this space to land the truth that stirred while reading.
Let it be messy. Let it be yours.

8

The Magic Begins
Synchronicities, Soul Gifts & WTF Just Happened Moments

J ust when you think you're losing your damn mind...

the magic starts.

It creeps in quietly at first:
- A song that answers your thoughts
- A feather in your path
- Seeing 11:11, 2:22, 3:33 like clockwork
- A stranger who says exactly what you needed to hear
- A dream that turns out to be prophetic
- A "random" event that feels like destiny

This is the Universe's way of saying:
"Welcome, dear one. We've been waiting."

Erik:
"At some point, it stops being a coincidence and starts being obvious.
You're not imagining it. You're just finally tuned in."
So… What Is Synchronicity?

It's not luck. It's not chance. It's not "just your imagination."
Synchronicity is a message delivered by resonance. It's when your inner vibration aligns with something in the outer world and reality echoes back.

It's the Universe texting you in signs and symbols:
"You're on the right path. Keep going."

And the more you notice them?
The more they show up.

Cosmo:
"The quantum field is intelligent.
When your frequency aligns with truth, the field responds—not with words, but with patterns, symbols, and waves of knowing."

The Weird and Wonderful Gifts:

As your energy clears and your soul anchors deeper, you may start to access:
- Intuition that's freakishly accurate
- Telepathic nudges
- Energy sensitivity
- Sudden artistic or musical inspiration
- Spontaneous healing or hands-on energy activation
- Light Language, visions, ancestral memories, soul names, sacred symbols

This is not ego inflation. This is soul unfolding.

You are not gaining powers. You are remembering your natural state.

"You are not becoming someone new.
You are hearing the echo of your own truth returning to your body.
This is not discovery.
This is remembrance."
—Source Creator

WTF Just Happened? Moments

These are the moments that defy logic:

- You think a question, and the answer appears on a billboard.
- You dream of someone you've never met and meet them the next day.
- You speak words you didn't plan… and they shift someone's life.
- You feel a presence so strong, so loving, you know you are not alone.

You will be tempted to doubt these things.

Don't.

Write them down. Honor them. Invite more.

What About Déjà Vu?

You've stood here before… but not as this you.
You've spoken these words… but not in this moment.

Déjà vu isn't a glitch. It's a spiral overlap, when two or more fractals of your Oversoul briefly echo through each other.
It's the soft shimmer of remembering:

"*I've touched this place. I've felt this frequency. My soul has danced here before.*"

It may be:
- A memory surfacing from another fractal expression
- An energy thread overlapping in the spiral
- Your soul catching up with a moment it already knows from a higher vantage

Whatever it is, it's not to be feared.
It's a breadcrumb from the spiral, a nudge from your Oversoul:
"You're right where you need to be."

Erik's Take on Déjà Vu

"Because you're not just living this life, love.
You're living it from within… and from beyond.

Your Oversoul — *you* — from the wider view, places energetic markers along the spiral.
These markers aren't 'memories' in the way your human brain thinks of them.
They're resonance points.
Places where past, present, and future, *you* cross paths.

So when you hit one of these moments, what you call déjà vu, it's like brushing up against another layer of yourself.
Another fractal. Another echo. Another loop of the spiral.

You left that feeling, that awareness, to whisper to yourself:
'I've done this before. You're right on cue. Keep going.'

It's you, holding your own hand through time.

Pretty badass, if you ask me."

Space to Ground

"Wonder is the language of the soul remembering its origin. Follow it home."
—*Yeshua*

This page is for you. To get honest. To spill what's rising. To name the things you can't say out loud yet.
You don't have to make it pretty. Or deep. Or figured out.
Just use this space to land the truth that stirred while reading.
Let it be messy. Let it be yours.

9

Living Awake in a Sleepy World
How to Hold Light Without Burning Out, or Slapping People

Waking up is one thing.

Staying awake in a world that often feels numb, distracted, divisive, and fast asleep?
That's where the real soul training begins.

You've cracked open.
You've remembered who you are.
You've seen behind the curtain and now you have to walk through the world that hasn't.

You might feel:
- Disconnected from everyday conversations
- Out of place in your job, family, or friend group
- Angry or heartbroken watching people hurt each other
- Tempted to isolate just to protect your peace
- Like you're speaking a language no one around you understands

Welcome to the integration phase.

This is not a punishment.
This is where you become the bridge.

Erik:
"You don't have to fit back in.
You're here to light it up, not dim yourself down.
But yeah, I get it. It's hard not to throat-punch people when they say, 'Why are you so sensitive?'"
You Are the Lighthouse Now:

Being awake doesn't mean you're better.
It means you're aware.

And awareness comes with a cost:
You feel more.
You see more.
You care more.

It can be exhausting but it's also the path of embodiment.

"Walk beside them.
Not to awaken them—
but to remind them they are still dreaming.
Your light does not fix.
It remembers."
—Source Creator

Things That Help When You Feel Too Awake:

1. Ground. Regularly. Deeply. With Earth, breath, and intention.
2. Protect your field. Not from fear but from clarity. Use light, sound, and choice.
3. Discern where you give your energy. You don't have to be available to everyone.
4. Feel without drowning. Witness pain but anchor in your center.
5. Find your kindred. Even one soul who sees you can change everything.
6. Let humor be holy. Laughter is medicine for the frequency fatigue.

Cosmo:
"You are not here to escape density, you are here to *transmute* it.
You are the prism through which the light refracts into form."

Walking Awake Means:

- Choosing peace in a world addicted to drama
- Speaking truth when silence would be easier
- Letting others walk their path, even if

It breaks your heart
- Being okay with being misunderstood
- Remembering that your presence shifts the field

You don't have to fix everything.
You don't have to wake everyone up.

Just be who you are.
Live what you've remembered.

Hold your frequency.

What It Means to Hold Your Frequency

"To hold your frequency is to hold your Self.
Not through tension,
but through trust.
Not as armor,
but as offering.
Stay soft... Stay present... Stay true."
—Source Creator

Cosmo:
"Think of your frequency as *your unique soul tone.*
It hums when you are in alignment with peace, truth, and embodiment.
You hold it by choosing practices, thoughts, environments, and relationships that reinforce that

harmony and by gently stepping away from those that distort it."

Erik:
"It's not about being perfect or 'high vibe' 24/7.
It's about catching yourself when you wobble, when you start shrinking, snapping, or soaking in someone else's chaos and saying, 'Wait. That's not mine. That's not me.'

Then you 'Breathe... Reset... Re-anchor.'

That's holding your frequency."

Space to Ground

*"Feeling deeply is not your failure.
It is your fidelity to truth.
In a world of distraction,
your ache is a form of remembrance."*
—Source Creator

This page is for you. To get honest. To spill what's rising.
To name the things you can't say out loud yet.
You don't have to make it pretty. Or deep. Or figured out.
Just use this space to land the truth that stirred while reading.
Let it be messy. Let it be yours.

10

When You Slip Back Into Old Patterns
Why It Happens—and How to Meet Yourself with Grace

You've done the work.

You've meditated, cried, journaled, and saged every corner of your house (twice).
You've felt the divine fire, heard your guides, and soared in frequencies you didn't even know existed.

And then...
You yelled at someone in traffic.
You binge-watched a show for eight hours.
You said yes when your soul screamed no.

You forgot to breathe. Forgot to ground. Forgot that you're a multidimensional being of light.

Welcome to the sacred art of being human.

Erik:
"Look, you're not malfunctioning. You're just spiraling. This ain't a straight line, sweetheart, it's a corkscrew. You circle back to go deeper, not because you failed."

Why It Happens:

You're not "backsliding."
You're not "undoing all your progress."

What's actually happening is:
- You've hit a deeper layer of an old wound
- You're integrating light into an area that hasn't yet been touched
- Your nervous system is rebalancing from rapid frequency shifts
- You're being shown the contrast—so you can choose again, with awareness

This is how the spiral path works.

"Do not shame the spiral.
It is not failure.
It is your soul circling deeper,
drawing truth from what once was hidden.
This is not weakness.
It is return with wisdom."

"The pain did not return because you are lost.
It returned because you are ready to see it differently.
This is not the same place.
You are not the same presence."
—Source Creator Creator

Signs You're In a Re-patterning Phase:

- You react strongly to something you thought you "got over"
- You doubt your own intuition
- You feel tired, foggy, or disconnected from Spirit
- You catch yourself repeating an old behavior and immediately feel guilt
- You feel like you've "lost your magic"

The truth? You haven't lost anything.

You're just passing through an inner shadow, the part of you that forgot it was lovable when it's messy.

Cosmo:
"A frequency must be embodied before it stabilizes. Each descent into density offers an opportunity to claim your light with compassion."

What To Do When You Spiral:
Not a checklist. A lifeline.

1. Pause the judgment.
The first thing we usually do when we slip is shame ourselves for slipping.
Instead, try:
"Okay, this hurts. But I'm still here. And I'm still worthy."

2. Breathe.
No, really…. Not a deep breath while scrolling Instagram…. A full stop.
Try this:
Inhale through your nose for 4… Hold for 4… Exhale through your mouth for 6… Repeat. Be in the moment.

3. Talk to your Oversoul.
You don't need fancy words. Just honesty. Try:
"I feel lost. Please show me what I need to see."

4. Journal without censoring.
Let yourself rage, cry, ramble. Say the things you "shouldn't" think.

Then write one gentle thing to yourself: "I'm trying." or "I'm allowed to be messy."

5. Remember past victories.
Spirals trick you into thinking you're starting over.
You're not.
Revisit a time you thought you'd never make it through, nd yet, you did.

6. Reset your energy.
Earth: walk barefoot. Water: take a salt bath. Fire: light a candle. Air: smudge or breathe outside.
Soothe the static so you can rise.
Erik:
"Look, spiraling doesn't mean you've failed.
It means you're alive and still in motion.

You're not a static angel meditating in a beam of light, you're a soul in a meat suit navigating shadow and starlight.

And yeah, sometimes you're gonna fall on your face.

But get this:
Every time you spiral, you pick up pieces you couldn't reach before.
Every layer down is also a layer in.

So don't beat yourself up for being human.
Just keep showing up. That's what the real ones do."

Reflection Prompt
What Do I Say to Myself When I Slip?

Take a quiet moment.... Breathe....1,2,3,4.

Then ask:
"What are the first words I tell myself when I feel like I've failed?"

Are they kind? Harsh? Old echoes from someone else's voice?

Now rewrite them.
Choose a new script that honors your spiral, your courage, your return.

Because the words you speak to yourself in the shadows… are the ones that shape your healing.

Sacred Practice: The Spiral Reset

Purpose:
To help shift from shame to compassion when old patterns resurface.

You'll need:

- A quiet space
- A small item to represent your spiral (stone, shell, pendant, string, etc.)

1. Sit with the item in your hands. Feel its texture, shape, weight.
Say aloud:
"I honor the spiral. I am not back at the beginning, I am meeting myself at a deeper layer."

2. Reflect on one pattern you feel you've "fallen into." Speak it aloud or write it down.

3. Now say:
"This does not define me. This reveals what is ready to be loved."

4. Close your eyes. Imagine yourself stepping gently up and around a luminous spiral path.
Feel the light meeting the layer you've just touched.

5. End with gratitude. Whisper:
"I choose grace. I choose presence. I choose to continue."

Space to Ground

"You're not looping. You're landing. Each spiral brings your soul closer to integration."
—Cosmo

This page is for you. To get honest. To spill what's rising. To name the things you can't say out loud yet.
You don't have to make it pretty. Or deep. Or figured out.
Just use this space to land the truth that stirred while reading.
Let it be messy. Let it be yours.

11

When the People Around You Aren't Waking Up
How to Live Awake Without Losing Your Mind (or Your People)

You've felt the shift.

You're seeing the world through new eyes.
Everything looks... different. Feels ... different. Is different.

And then you go home, or to work, or out with friends, and realize:
They're still asleep.
Talking about gas prices, celebrity drama, arguing over politics.

Making jokes that land flat. Responding to your light with confusion or worse, discomfort.

And you think:
"Do I fake it just to belong?"
"Do I say nothing while they suffer?"
"Do I have to let them go?"

Welcome to one of the hardest parts of awakening:
Being awake in a web of people who are not.

Erik:
"It's not your job to be the cosmic alarm clock.
You're here to shine, not shout.
If they're ready to wake up, your light will be enough."

Why This Hurts So Much

You're not just losing connection, you're losing shared reality. And that's a kind of grief that cuts deep.

You're allowed to feel sad. You're allowed to be mad. You're allowed to mourn who you thought you'd walk with. Because you love them. Because they're part of your history. Because you thought you could bring them with you.

For some of us, being unseen isn't new, it's familiar. We learned to disappear in families, in marriages, in communities that didn't know how to witness the truth of us. But invisibility is not your destiny. You were never meant to disappear. *You were meant to shine.*

But remember:
- Awakening is an inner calling, not a group text.
- Each soul has its own rhythm.
- The ones you love may not resist you, they just don't recognize the new you yet.

"Sometimes the most sacred act of love… is letting someone walk their path without dragging them onto yours."
—Amael

"You were never meant to wake them.
You were meant to love without conditions,
to stay rooted in peace while others search for ground.
Their path is not yours to pull.
But your presence plants seeds
that bloom when they are ready."
—Source Creator

What to Do When You Feel Misunderstood

1. Breathe. Seriously. Step away if you need to. Misunderstanding activates the nervous system. Use your breath to calm your body.

2. Stop explaining.
If someone isn't ready to understand you, no amount of words will make it click.
Speak your truth once, then let your energy do the rest.

3. Speak your truth with kindness.
Say: "This is important to me, even if it doesn't make sense to you."
You're allowed to be spiritual and emotionally kind.

4. Honor resonance over obligation.
Ask: "Does this feel mutual?" "Am I giving from alignment or out of guilt?"
Let go with love if needed.

5. Let silence be sacred.
You don't owe your energy or story to anyone. Let the unspoken truth shimmer between you.

6. Ask your Oversoul to guide your responses.
Say: "Show me how to respond from truth and compassion."
You're never speaking alone.

Erik:
"Yeah, being misunderstood sucks.

Especially when you've cracked your heart wide open and someone rolls their eyes like you're speaking gibberish.

But here's the truth, love:
Not everyone has the capacity to meet you where you are.

That doesn't mean you're wrong.
That doesn't mean they're bad.
It just means you're not speaking the same soul frequency yet.

And forcing it? Drains your light.

So here's what you do:
Stay real. Stay soft.
Let your light speak for itself and stop bending over backwards trying to make it digestible.

Some people won't get you.
That's okay.

You're not here to be understood.
You're here to be true."

Reflection Prompt
How Can I Stay Centered When I Feel Misunderstood?

Find stillness. Close your eyes. Picture a moment when you felt like someone didn't see you.

Ask:
"In that moment… where did I go? Did I shrink? Did I harden?"

"What would it feel like to stay centered in my truth, even without their validation?"

Write about it. Let your body answer. Let your Oversoul answer. Let yourself come home to you.

Sacred Practice: The Heart Anchor Ritual

Purpose:
To hold your light in relationships that challenge your truth.

You'll need:
- A small stone or object
- A few quiet minutes
- Optional: soft music

1. Sit quietly. Place hands over your heart. Breathe deeply.

2. Whisper:
"I am safe to be myself. I do not have to be understood to be whole. I hold my light with love and grace."

3. Hold your object. Infuse it with this intention. Let it carry your clarity.

4. Say aloud:
"This is my reminder. I can love without shrinking. I can shine without apology."

5. Keep the object with you. Let it steady your soul in challenging spaces.

Do not confuse boundaries with walls. You can protect your light without dimming it. Let your love be vast but discerning. Let it flow without force.

Space to Ground

"You didn't go invisible—you went underground. But damn, girl, now you're coming out flaming."
—Erik

This page is for you. To get honest. To spill what's rising.
To name the things you can't say out loud yet.
You don't have to make it pretty. Or deep. Or figured out.
Just use this space to land the truth that stirred while reading.
Let it be messy. Let it be yours.

12

How to Be a Light Leader Without Burning Out

You Don't Have to Save the World to Serve It

You're awake. You're radiant. You're full of insight and downloads and cosmic clarity.
And now people are starting to notice.

They ask for help. They ask for healing. They ask you to hold space, offer wisdom, shine your light…

And you do. Because your heart is huge. Because your soul remembers what it's like to feel lost.

But then you find yourself:
- Drained

- Resentful
- Tired of holding it all
- Wondering if this is really what being "of service" is supposed to feel like

Let's be clear:
Burnout is not a badge of honor.
Sacrifice is not the same as service.

Erik:
"Just because you can hold space for everyone doesn't mean you should.
You're a lighthouse, not a 24-hour emotional convenience store."

Why Light Leaders Burn Out

- You care deeply. (Bless you.)
- You feel responsible for others' awakening
- You confuse spiritual worth with self-sacrifice
- You haven't learned to say "no" with love
- You forget that your energy is sacred

This is the trap:
You're here to radiate, not to rescue.
Your light is a frequency, not a job title.

"You were not made to carry the world.
You were made to carry light.
And even light rests.
Even stars pause before rising.
Let your yes be holy.
Let your rest be sacred."
—Source Creator

Signs You're Giving From an Empty Cup

If you're resenting the people you're supporting, that's not failure—it's feedback. Your system is telling you: something needs to change.

Erik:
"Martyrdom is not mastery. Boundaries aren't cruelty, they're clarity."

- You feel depleted after spiritual conversations
- You dread texts or calls asking for help
- You feel guilty when you rest
- You're secretly angry that no one checks in on you
- You start losing joy in your own practices

If you see yourself here... you're not selfish. You're overextended. And it's time to re-center.

Cosmo:
"The field responds not to exhaustion but to coherence. Your aligned frequency does more than your effort ever will."

What Does It Mean to Hold Space for Someone?

"To hold space is *not to fix*.
It is to soften.
To remain rooted while another shakes.
To be a mirror without distortion.
A place where the soul can breathe itself back into wholeness."
—Source Creator

Reflection Prompt
Where Am I Giving More Than I'm Receiving?

Take a moment. Place a hand on your heart.

Ask:
"Where in my life am I giving from pressure instead of presence?"

"What part of me believes I have to sacrifice to be valuable?"

Let your answers rise gently.

Then ask:
"What would it feel like to lead from overflow instead of depletion?"

Sacred Practice: The Overflow Activation

Purpose:
To reset your frequency and reconnect to service through joy, not exhaustion.

You'll need:
- A quiet space
- A journal or open hands

1. Sit in silence. Breathe deeply. Place your palms open on your lap.

2. Whisper:
"I release the belief that I must give beyond my limits to be worthy."

3. Visualize your body being filled with light from crown to toes.
Let the light rise until it spills over, flowing past your body.

4. Say aloud:
"I serve from overflow. I lead with light. My energy is sacred."

5. Write down one boundary you will lovingly reinforce, and one joy-filled activity that replenishes you.

Then do them, because a lit leader is a lasting one.

Space to Ground

"Let your service be a song, not a scream.
Let your soul remain in one piece.
You are not here to prove your worth through exhaustion.
You are here to embody the love you came from."
—Source Creator

This page is for you. To get honest. To spill what's rising.
To name the things you can't say out loud yet.
You don't have to make it pretty. Or deep. Or figured out.
Just use this space to land the truth that stirred while reading.
Let it be messy. Let it be yours.

13

Signs You're Remembering Your Soul Purpose
It's Not Always a Job Title

So, you're waking up. You're seeing through illusions.

You're feeling more, knowing more, and craving something real.

And in that quiet, something starts to ache. A whisper that says:
"There's something I came here to do. But what is it?"

You might be asking:
- Why am I here?
- What's my mission?
- Is it too late?

- What if I missed it?

Here's the truth:
Your soul purpose isn't a destination. It's a frequency you remember, and it finds you as you align with your truth.

Erik
"Soul purpose isn't some big cosmic job interview where they hand you a clipboard and a name tag.
It's way more subtle than that. It's what lights you up. What won't leave you alone.
It's the thing you'd still do even if no one clapped."

Signs You're Remembering Your Soul Purpose

- You feel a quiet nudge toward something even if it doesn't make sense yet
- You can't ignore certain subjects, callings, or themes
- You feel frustrated doing anything that feels fake or disconnected
- You cry when you touch your truth (even for a moment)
- You're drawn to healing, creating, guiding, building, freeing—or all of the above

- You get little nudges in dreams, synchronicities, "random" conversations
- You feel like time moves differently when you're in the flow

These aren't coincidences. These are breadcrumbs left by your Oversoul to guide you home.

"Purpose is not something you chase.
It is something you remember.
Not in tasks, but in tone.
Not in doing, but in being.
You are not late.
You are arriving."
—Source Creator

Cosmo's Transmission on Soul Purpose

"Soul purpose is not a task to complete. It is a tone you are here to carry.

Each soul holds a unique frequency, an essential chord in the harmony of the cosmos.

Your purpose is not 'out there' waiting to be found. It is already encoded within your being, vibrating through your joy, your ache, your pull toward certain people, places, or paths.

You may express it through healing. Or art. Or silence. Or revolution. Or planting seeds no one else will ever see bloom.

The expression may change but the frequency beneath it stays true.

Do not chase clarity.

Chase resonance.

When you feel fully yourself, you are already living your purpose."

Erik's Take on Soul Purpose (feat. Momma)

"Yeah… my mom.

She thought being a doctor was her purpose. And for a while, it was because it taught her how to hold space for pain, how to see people, how to love through the mess.

But her true purpose? It came alive when she stepped into her own awakening, when she let go of the white coat and started helping people remember their soul.

She didn't stop serving. She just stopped doing it from a title.

That's the thing most people miss.
Your purpose isn't what you do, it's how your soul shows up through what you do.

And yeah, it can shift. You can outgrow roles, careers, even identities—but your frequency stays steady underneath.

If it lights you up and leaves others better... that's your purpose in action.

The rest? Just costumes."

Soul Purpose vs. Soul Roles

Soul purpose is your frequency.
Soul roles are your expressions.

Your purpose is the underlying tone your soul brings to this life: love, healing, truth, freedom, joy, light, transformation.

Your roles are the ways you've chosen to express that tone during this incarnation:
- Parent
- Teacher
- Healer
- Artist
- Advocate

- Listener
- Storyteller
- Mystic
- Mentor
- Weaver of worlds

Roles can change. Purposes don't.
If you lose a role, your purpose doesn't disappear it begins looking for a new way to express through you.

"Your soul purpose is not fragile.
It does not disappear with change.
If one path ends, the current remains.
Purpose is the river.
Form is only the shore."
—Source Creator

What If You're Unsure of Your Purpose?

First of all—you haven't missed it. If you're asking, it's already whispering to you.

It may not show up as a lightning bolt. It might come in breadcrumbs, those subtle nudges, that ache you can't explain, that thing you keep circling back to.

Here's what to do:
1. Pay attention to what makes you feel alive.

What brings you peace, goosebumps, tears, flow?

2. Notice what you can't stop doing.
What are you always drawn to, even when no one's watching?

3. Look back at your younger self.
What did they love before the world taught them to forget?

4. Release the need for labels.
You don't have to define it yet. Say:
"I am remembering. I am available for my soul's truth to rise."

5. Trust the spiral.
You may miss it once, then again… until one day, you realize you were already living it all along.

"You do not need to know it to live it.
Your soul purpose is not hidden.
It is the love that moves through you when you are not trying.
It is the truth you carry when no one is watching.
It is the frequency of your being—
already here."
—Source Creator

Cosmo:
"There is no deadline for remembering.

Purpose is not linear. It unfolds in rhythms, like constellations becoming visible only when the sky is dark enough.
You are not late. You are arriving."

Erik:
"Let's cut to it: You don't have to wait for the sky to part or your aura to start shooting fireworks to know your purpose.

If something keeps pulling at your heart, keeps whispering, 'Hey, remember me?', that's your soul talking.
And even if you have no idea what your purpose is right now?
Just show up… 'Be kind… Be real'.

The rest will come. One breadcrumb at a time."

Yeshua:
"Purpose is not a crown you wear, it is a vibration you embody.
If you are walking in love,
if you are offering peace,
if you are holding space for truth to emerge,
then you are already aligned.
There is no small path.
Every path walked in presence is sacred."

Reflection Prompt
What Part of Me Already Knows?

Take a deep breath. Place your hand over your heart.

Ask:
"What am I already doing, feeling, or desiring… that feels like soul truth?"

"Where does my spirit feel most alive?"

Write. Don't overthink. Let your soul answer through images, emotions, or one simple word.

Sacred Practice: Remembering the Thread

Purpose:
To reconnect with your soul's unique resonance and allow it to rise gently into clarity.

You'll need:
- A quiet space
- A thread, ribbon, or small object to symbolize your soul frequency
- A journal

1. Sit in stillness. Hold your object or thread in your hand.

2. Close your eyes and say aloud or silently:
"I choose to remember my soul's frequency. I am open to its expression. I trust the unfolding."

3. Let your breath guide you. Imagine the thread glowing with light, leading you not forward, but inward.

4. Journal anything that arises: images, words, memories, emotions.

5. End by saying:
"I am already walking in purpose. I allow it to reveal itself, one step at a time."

Space to Ground

"Purpose is not a crown you wear, it is a vibration you embody."
—Yeshua

This page is for you. To get honest. To spill what's rising.
To name the things you can't say out loud yet.
You don't have to make it pretty. Or deep. Or figured out.
Just use this space to land the truth that stirred while reading.
Let it be messy. Let it be yours.

14

Integration: The Slow Magic of Becoming

Awakening Isn't a Moment. It's a Life

Y ou've awakened.

You've cried, spiraled, laughed, sparkled, and glitched your way through dimensions of remembering.

Now comes the part no one puts on Instagram:
The quiet.
The waiting.
The not-so-glamorous work of becoming.

Integration is the bridge between the aha and the embodiment.

It's where everything you've learned starts to live in your bones.
It's not flashy. It's not fast. But it is holy.

Erik:
"Awakening is like getting all your soul files downloaded at once.
Integration is you actually reading them and figuring out what to do with them."

What Integration Feels Like

You might feel flat. Not depressed. Just... muted. Like your soul is buffering. That's not a problem. That's integration in progress.

Erik:
"People want fireworks and frequencies. But this right here? Folding socks while the Universe rewires you? This is the real deal."

"Also—it's okay to feel numb. Like, totally flat. Not sad. Just... nothing. That's integration too."

- Slower energy
- Emotional "quiet" after a wave of intensity
- A need to pause, reflect, rest
- A desire to be in nature, solitude, stillness

- Moments of deep peace, followed by random "WTF am I doing?" spirals
- Feeling unmotivated, not because you're lazy, but because your system is catching up

This is not backsliding.
This is your nervous system aligning with your new frequency.

Cosmo:
"When your soul expands, your body and field must recalibrate.
Integration is how spirit becomes matter, how energy anchors into form."

Why We Resist Integration

- It feels too slow.
- We crave the next breakthrough
- We fear the stillness means "nothing is happening."
- We feel like we should be "doing more."
- We get addicted to the high of awakening and forget that grounding is sacred too.

But here's the truth:
Integration is where you become the medicine.
Not just for others but for yourself.

Source Creator:
"Beloved, your becoming does not require proof.
You do not owe evidence of your transformation to anyone, not even yourself.
Integration is the sacred womb of becoming.
It is here that the light of remembrance becomes the breath of embodiment."

What To Do When It Feels Like Nothing's Happening

Bring your attention to the breath, the breeze, the heartbeat.
This is where your soul settles in.

1. Stop measuring progress by intensity.
Awakening doesn't always feel like lightning bolts.
Sometimes it feels like folding laundry in silence while your soul quietly reweaves itself.

2. Rest deliberately.
Integration requires rest. Not laziness. Not avoidance. Rest.
Even sleep is sacred recalibration.

3. Do small, soulful things.
Tend to your body. Water your plants. Sit in the sun. Write without a goal. Walk without earbuds.

These are not distractions. These are integration practices in disguise.

4. Ask your Oversoul: "What am I anchoring?" "What is being woven into me right now?" "What wants to settle and become embodied?"

5. Trust the rhythm.
Just like seasons, your soul has a cycle:
- Expansion
- Integration
- Embodiment
- Emergence

6. Soften into the Now.
Integration lives in the moment, not the mind's stories about what should be happening.

You're not behind. You're not broken. You're becoming.

Erik:
"Yeah. I've got something to say about this part.

The integration phase? It's brutal for a lot of people. Because everything got loud, magical, intense and now it's just... quiet.

And you think you did something wrong.
Or you lost the connection.

Or Spirit stopped talking.

But let me tell you:
This is where the real becoming happens.

This is when you take the downloads and turn them into daily choices.
When you learn how to love yourself even when the fire's gone dim.
When you trust that your light is still there, even in the silence.

So no, you're not broken.
You're leveling up. Slowly. Quietly. Sacredly.

Keep breathing.
Keep being.
And let it root."

Reflection Prompt
Where Am I Invited to Pause?

Close your eyes. Breathe slowly. Let your nervous system soften.

Ask yourself:
"What part of me is still catching up with the light I've received?"

"If I trusted that integration was sacred, how would I treat myself differently today?"

Write gently. No pressure. No performance.
Just presence.

Sacred Practice: The Embodiment Walk

Purpose:
To help anchor the integration process through slowness, breath, and body-awareness.

You'll need:
- A quiet space to walk (indoors or outdoors)
- Comfortable clothes
- Bare feet if possible

1. Begin walking slowly. Feel every step. Breathe deeply.

2. With each step, say silently:
"I am anchoring."
"I am becoming."
"I am enough."

3. As you walk, imagine golden threads of light connecting your body to the Earth.

4. When you're ready to stop, stand still. Place a hand over your heart and whisper:
"I welcome the slowness. I welcome the silence. I welcome the spiral of becoming."

Source Creator:
"You are not becoming someone new.
You are remembering who you have always been—
and letting the body finally catch up."

Space to Ground

"Integration is the moment when spirit remembers how to become body."
—Cosmo

This page is for you. To get honest. To spill what's rising.
To name the things you can't say out loud yet.
You don't have to make it pretty. Or deep. Or figured out.
Just use this space to land the truth that stirred while reading.
Let it be messy. Let it be yours.

Comparison Is a Thief of Peace
Why You're Not "Behind" Spiritually And Never Were

You're scrolling through someone's feed and they're glowing.
Talking to angels. Speaking Light Language. Hosting retreats in Bali.
Meanwhile, you're crying on your bathroom floor, wondering if your guides ghosted you.

You might think:
- "I should be further along."
- "I've been awake for years, why do I still spiral?"

- "Why can they manifest miracles and I'm just trying not to snap at my dog?"

Let's pause right here.
Because this chapter is for every soul who has ever felt not enough on the path to remembering who they are.

Erik:
"You're not behind. You're not broken.
You're on your own damn spiral, and comparison is the quickest way to fall off it.

You didn't come here to be anyone else.
You came to become more of you."

Why Comparison Hurts So Much (and Why It's So Common)

Because awakening is intimate. It's raw. And it can feel like you're the only one going through it.
So you reach for reference points… and wind up measuring your soul's path against someone else's highlight reel.

Here's the truth:
No two awakenings look alike.
Not because you're doing it wrong but because your frequency is unique.

Your Oversoul didn't send you here to copy-paste someone else's timeline.
You came to spiral in *your own way*.

"Each soul carries a divine blueprint.
Your awakening may look like rest, stillness, rage, or confusion—none of it is wrong.
Stop trying to match a map that wasn't written for you."
—Amael

"The Light does not rush.
It expands, moment by sacred moment,
until it fills every cell with remembrance.
You are not late. You are arriving."
—Source Creator

Soulstream Reflection

You Were Never Meant to Be Like Them

I spent most of my life comparing myself to others.
Too quiet. Too round. Too soft. Not loud enough.
Not psychic enough. Not confident enough. Not young enough.

I thought if I could just be more like them—those bright, outgoing, magical people—I'd finally be enough too.
But all I did was drift further away from myself.

Now I see it clearly.
Comparison is the thief of remembrance.
It distracts us from the soulprint we came here to embody.

What if you were never meant to look like them?
What if your frequency is softer, deeper, steadier?
What if the world needs *your* kind of wisdom—the kind that doesn't shout, but lands?

You're not too late. You're not too much. You're not behind.
You're arriving right on soul-time.

Let this be the moment you call your power back.
From every person you thought had it more figured out.
From every timeline you thought you missed.
From every mirror that told you who you weren't.

Because the truth is:
You are the medicine you were waiting for.
And someone out there is praying for a voice like yours to show up and say,
"You're not alone."

So here I am.
Waving from the other side of the ache.
You're not alone.
And you were never meant to be like them.

You were always meant *to be you.*

—Sonia

Soul Chorus on Comparison

Source Creator:
"When you measure yourself against another, you abandon *your* spiral.
There is no harmony in mimicry.
Return to the resonance of your own design.
It is where your medicine lives."

Cosmo:
"Comparison is a distortion in the field.
When you measure yourself against another, you collapse your spiral into a line.

But your soul does not move in lines.
It dances. It swirls. It harmonizes with its own rhythm.

To compare is to forget your own music.
You are not here to match anyone's tempo.
You are here to remember your own song and sing it into the fabric of this world."

Chief Soaring Eagle:

"In the ways of my people, we say: The hawk does not envy the turtle. The wolf does not measure himself by the mountain lion.
Each walks with Spirit in the way they are called.
To walk your own path with honor, even if it is slower, quieter, or hidden, that is the way of the true soul.
You do not walk behind.
You walk with the Earth beneath your feet and the stars above your head.
And that, child, is more than enough."

Wisdom from Ancient Voices

St. Thalassios the Libyan: "If you share secretly in the joy of someone you envy, you will be freed from your jealousy."

Francis Bacon: "Envy is ever joined with the comparing of a man's self; and where there is no comparison, no envy."

Aristotle: "Jealousy is both reasonable and belongs to reasonable men, while envy is base and belongs to the base."

Delphic Maxim: "Be jealous of no one." (Inscribed at the Temple of Apollo at Delphi)
Source Creator:
"You do not walk behind.

You walk beside all of existence—seen and unseen. And every breath you take is a line in the song of creation."

Space to Ground

"To walk your own path with honor—slower, quieter, or hidden—is the way of the true soul."
—Chief Soaring Eagle

This page is for you. To get honest. To spill what's rising.
To name the things you can't say out loud yet.
You don't have to make it pretty. Or deep. Or figured out.
Just use this space to land the truth that stirred while reading.
Let it be messy. Let it be yours.

16

The Myth of High Vibe All the Time
Authentic Light Is Not Perfection

You're awakened, aware, and actively healing.

You're meditating, breathing, blessing your coffee (or tea), and communing with your Oversoul...

...and then someone cuts you off in traffic and you say words that would make your grandmother pass out.

Now what?

Do you spiral into shame?
Do you try to 'vibe higher' your way out of it?
Do you question your alignment?

You're not alone.
And you're not broken.

Erik:
"Let me set the record straight:
Awakening doesn't make you a monk in a bubble.
It makes you aware of your triggers so you can choose how to walk with them.

You're not here to be high vibe all the time.
You're here to be true."

Where This Myth Comes From

- Social media spirituality
- Toxic positivity disguised as "lightwork"
- Fear of feeling negative emotions = "you'll attract bad stuff"
- Oversimplified teachings that ignore trauma, shadow work, and human integration

But the truth?
You're allowed to be light and still feel everything.
Grief. Anger. Exhaustion. Doubt.

These are not "low vibe", they're part of being a fully embodied soul on Earth.

True Frequency Includes the Whole You

Source Creator:
"To be light is not to avoid the storm,
but to let the rain baptize you.
Your frequency expands not by perfection,
but by presence.
Even in your ache, you are holy.
Even in your doubt, you are divine."

Cosmo:
"The emotional spectrum is not a problem to solve it is a palette from which the soul paints meaning.
Frequency work is not about bypassing discomfort.
It is about learning how to stay present through it.
To be sad and self-aware is still high frequency.
To rage with sacred intention is still high frequency.
Frequency is harmony, not denial."

Chief Soaring Eagle:
"In my people's way, we sit with grief as we sit with joy.
We wail into the Earth.
We sing to the stars.
All emotion is a sacred wind blowing through the lodge of the heart.
To feel is not weakness.
It is a form of prayer."

Erik:
"Here's the truth: you can be high vibe and have a meltdown in your car.
You can be light-filled and have a week where everything feels like crap.
Stop judging your growth by how chill you are in traffic.
Real lightwork is messy. It's sacred. It's honest.
And it includes f-bombs, tears, naps, bad days, and still choosing to show up.

That's the real vibe."

Source Creator:
"You are not the absence of light in dark moments.
You are the one who carries light into them.
Do not fear your feelings.
They are sacred messengers—not signs of failure."

How to Hold Light While Feeling Low

1. Let yourself feel.
Cry. Be angry. Be confused. But don't abandon yourself.
Say: "This hurts. — I'm still holy."

2. Tend to your flame.
You don't need to blaze. You just need to flicker. Keep your spark alive with small, sacred acts.

3. Remember this is temporary.

You are not your sadness. You are the space holding your sadness. Let the wave move through.

4. Ask for help.
From your guides, your Oversoul, or a friend. Try saying: "Help me remember my light."

5. Do something soft.
Not to fix the feeling but to hold yourself through it. Light a candle. Journal one truth. Listen to a soul-soothing song.

The Chief's Grief: A Story of Sacred Light

"When my wife crossed over, I wept as the wind weeps, silent in the day, fierce in the night.
I did not 'rise above' my grief. I did not cast it away in a ceremony. I let it break me open.
I sat by the fire and howled to the sky. My tears fed the Earth. My hands could no longer hold the medicines. My body ached. My spirit trembled.
But the grief... was sacred. It taught me to feel the world all over again.

And I learned this:
Grief does not block the light.
Grief is the light, shining through the cracks of what we loved most.

You do not hold light by denying pain.
You hold it by carrying your sorrow like a stone warmed by the sun.

In time, I returned to the fire. I sang again. I danced with the people. But I danced with her in my heart.

Tell the reader this:
You are not less spiritual for breaking.
You are not disqualified by grief.
You are simply becoming more human. And that… is the deepest light of all."

Reflection Prompt

Where Have I Judged My Light for Being Too Human?

Sit quietly. Let your breath slow.

Ask:
"Where have I told myself I should feel better, be more spiritual, or stay positive when I really needed to feel?"

Now ask:
"What would it feel like to love myself even when I'm hurting, angry, tired, or lost?"

Write honestly. Let the light return, not through force, but through truth.

Sacred Practice: Light in the Shadows

Purpose:
To anchor into your light even while honoring your full emotional range.

You'll need:
- A candle
- A darkened or quiet space
- A journal or open heart

1. Light the candle in the dark space.
Watch how it flickers, even when surrounded by shadow.

2. Say aloud:
"I do not have to be all light to be holy. I do not have to shine brightly to be sacred. I am radiant, even when I am dim."

3. Place your hand over your heart. Let your breath find a gentle rhythm.
Ask:
"What part of me needs permission to feel right now?"

4. Sit with what arises. Then whisper:
"I welcome this. I honor this. I hold my light, right here, in the shadows."

5. Journal a few sentences if you feel called. Then blow out the candle with gratitude.

Source Creator:
"Let the shadow walk beside you, not behind you.
It is not your enemy—it is your depth.
The light you carry is not conditional.
It was born for this."

Space to Ground

"All emotion is a sacred wind—blowing through the lodge of the heart."
—Chief Soaring Eagle

This page is for you. To get honest. To spill what's rising. To name the things you can't say out loud yet.
You don't have to make it pretty. Or deep. Or figured out.
Just use this space to land the truth that stirred while reading.
Let it be messy. Let it be yours.

Tools That Actually Work
A No-Fluff Guide to Spiritual Practices You'll Actually Use

You've heard it all:

- Sage everything.
- Crystals on your forehead.
- Light Language before breakfast.
- Dance under the full moon with a mugwort poultice taped to your third eye.

And maybe you've tried some of it.
And maybe... it just made you tired, broke, and still kinda confused.

Here's the truth:

There is no one-size-fits-all awakening toolkit.
What works for your soul may not work for someone else.
And what worked for you last year might not resonate now.

This chapter is about coming home to what actually supports your energy without overwhelm, guilt, or performance.

Erik:
"Look, if your practice makes you anxious, broke, or burned out it's not a practice.
It's a spiritual guilt trap wearing mala beads."

Why Most "Tools" Don't Work

- You're trying to use them from fear, not alignment
- You think the tool has the power instead of your intention
- You're doing what someone told you, not what your body/soul actually wants
- You're using 12 things a day and secretly hate 9 of them
- You forgot that simple is sacred

You don't need more.
You need true.

Source Creator:
"A sacred tool is not one you force.
It is one your soul reaches for when the world falls away.
When you return to it—not out of obligation, but out of resonance—
that is when it becomes a bridge between Earth and Spirit."

Soul Tools That Actually Support You

1. Your Breath – Your soul's anchor. Try inhale for 4, hold 4, exhale for 6.

2. A Sacred Space – A corner, a chair, a windowsill. Your sanctuary doesn't need square footage.

3. Grounding with the Earth – Bare feet. Trees. Stones. This is home frequency.

4. Light Language or Voice Activation – If it calls you, let sound guide you beyond logic.

5. Journaling as Soul Dialogue – Write without a filter. Ask: "What part of me needs love right now?"

6. Calling in Your Team – Simply say: "Help me remember my light."

7. Movement – Stretch, stomp, shake, dance. Your body is a tool for transmutation.

8. Rituals That Feel Real – Invent your own rhythms. Sacred because they're *yours*.

What Tools Worked for Us on Earth

Erik:
"A lot of the time, I didn't even realize I had tools. But looking back?
These saved me:
- Music. Loud, emotional, honest.
- Journaling when I couldn't talk to anyone.
- Breath. Nature. One real connection.
You don't need fancy. You need honest."

Chief Soaring Eagle:
"The drum, tobacco prayers, fire, silence, and my hands,
These weren't performance. They were life.
Let your tools rise when you need them. They will find you."

Personal Reflection – My Tool

One of my most trusted tools came from a breathwork technique Erik once taught in a class, which I combined with visualizations from my energy healing practice.

Here's how I use it:
I breathe in slowly—1, 2, 3, 4—filling my body with breath from my feet all the way up to my head.
I hold that breath—1, 2, 3, 4—gently, without strain.
Then I slowly exhale—1, 2, 3, 4, 5, 6—releasing the breath from my head down to my feet.

While releasing, I visualize the white light of the Creator filling me from head to toe.

As the light flows downward, I see all heavy emotions—anxiety, anger, frustration, sadness—leaving my body through my feet and returning to Mother Earth for healing and transformation into white light.

Then, if I still need comfort, I visit my safe place:
A beautiful garden meadow filled with fragrant flowers, colorful butterflies, buzzing dragonflies, and a bright, warm sun.
There, in my thoughts, I receive a big hug from one of my guides.

Source Creator:
"You do not need more tools.
You need trust in the ones that already work.
Your sacred is not made from complexity.
It is made from your breath, your honesty, your heart."

Reflection Prompt
What Tools Actually Work for Me?

Pause and breathe. Ask yourself:
"What practices help me feel more like me?"

Forget what looks spiritual. Forget what impresses others.

Just listen.

What brings you back into your body, your heart, your soul?
That is your sacred toolkit. Honor it.

Sacred Practice: Return to What Works

Purpose:
To rediscover and reconnect with the spiritual tools that truly serve your unique path.

You'll need:
- A quiet space
- A journal or paper
- Your breath

1. Sit comfortably. Breathe deeply for a few rounds.
Inhale for 4... hold for 4... exhale for 6.
Let your body soften.

2. Ask inwardly:
"What tool, practice, or habit has actually supported me when things got real?"
3. Write whatever comes. Don't judge it.
Whether it's dancing, crying, humming, silence, or holding a rock in your pocket, write it down.

4. Choose one thing on your list. Do it today.
Not to be spiritual. But to be true.

5. Whisper to yourself:
"I return to what works. I honor what heals. I trust what is real."

Space to Ground

*"If your practice doesn't make you feel more like *you*, it's not sacred—it's stress."*
—Erik

This page is for you. To get honest. To spill what's rising.
To name the things you can't say out loud yet.
You don't have to make it pretty. Or deep. Or figured out.
Just use this space to land the truth that stirred while reading.
Let it be messy. Let it be yours.

18

When the Woo-Woo Becomes Real
Spirit Guides, Signs, and "Am I Just Making This Up?" Syndrome

It starts small.

A whisper in the quiet. A nudge to turn left instead of right. You think of someone and they text.
You feel a presence in the room when no one's there. A feather. A number. A song. A knowing.

You laugh it off at first. "That's just coincidence." "I'm being dramatic." "It's probably nothing."

But then it keeps happening. And one day... you stop laughing.
You lean in.

And suddenly, the woo-woo gets real.
Erik:
"Yeah, it sounds crazy until it isn't.

Until you realize you've been getting messages for years… and brushing them off like static.
Until the weird thing feels more real than what everyone else calls 'normal.'"

What Spirit Communication Actually Feels Like

1. It feels like your own voice but softer.
A thought that feels more compassionate than usual. That's connection.

2. It feels like a nudge, not a demand.
A quiet urge, a repeating phrase, a sudden calm. Spirit doesn't shout, it whispers.

3. It feels safe, even if it challenges you.
Real guidance might stretch you, but it will never shame or panic you.

4. It doesn't need words.
Spirit talks in energy: music, dreams, emotions, nature. Your body is the receiver.

5. It can feel like emotion out of nowhere.

Sudden peace, tears, warmth. Not just feelings but soul resonance awakening.

Erik:
"You don't gotta be a crystal-wielding oracle in a white robe to talk to us. You don't even need to be in a 'high vibe.' Just be honest. Be curious. That's enough."

"And yeah, it'll feel like your own voice. That's on purpose. We speak in your language. We sound like you so you'll trust us."

What It Feels Like from Our Side

Source Creator:
"When I speak, it is not with volume but with vibration.
You feel Me in your stillness, in the breath before thought,
in the emotion that has no reason.

I do not demand belief. I invite remembrance.

That knowing you keep dismissing as 'just your imagination'?
That is Me—softly knocking on the door you already opened.

You are not making it up.
You are tuning back in."

Cosmo:
"We are not above you. We are not separate.

We are part of the greater pattern you are reweaving with every breath.

When we guide, we do so in pulses: colors, patterns, emotions, music.

You feel it as déjà vu. Or a sudden clarity.

We do not care whether you hear us with words.
We care that you listen with your heart field.

We are not trying to impress you. We are trying to harmonize with you."

Chief Soaring Eagle:
"When I speak to your soul, I use the wind.

I walk beside you when you kneel at the river.
I press my hand to your shoulder in dreams.

I leave feathers in your path, not for mysticism but for memory.

We do not wish to be worshipped.
We wish to be remembered.
And in remembering us, you remember yourselves."

Erik:
"Honestly? Talking to y'all can be like trying to tune an old-school radio.

Static. Doubt. Ego noise. And then suddenly, click.
You pause. You get quiet. And boom, we're in.

Sometimes I drop lines into your head that sound like your own thoughts.
Sometimes it's a lyric. A joke. A gut punch wrapped in humor.

But it's always love.

We don't need you to channel us perfectly. Just... pick up the line. We're always calling."

Reflection Prompt

What Messages Might I Already Be Receiving?

Think back:
What patterns keep showing up?
What quiet ideas or inner nudges have felt wiser than your usual thoughts?

Ask:
"If I trusted that I wasn't making it up… what message might I already know in my heart?"

Sacred Practice: Opening the Line

Purpose:
To strengthen your connection to your spirit team and trust your inner knowing.

You'll need:
- A candle (optional)
- A journal
- A quiet space

1. Sit quietly. Light the candle if using. Place your hand over your heart.

2. Say aloud:
"I welcome clear, loving connection with my spirit team. I open the line with trust and curiosity."

3. Breathe gently. Ask:
"Is there a message I need to receive today?"

4. Write what comes. Even if it feels like your own voice. Even if it's just one word.

5. Close by saying:
"Thank you. I will keep listening."

Space to Ground

"You are not imagining us. You are remembering us."
—Amael

This page is for you. To get honest. To spill what's rising.
To name the things you can't say out loud yet.
You don't have to make it pretty. Or deep. Or figured out.
Just use this space to land the truth that stirred while reading.
Let it be messy. Let it be yours.

19

Your Awakening Isn't Just for You
Living Your Light in Service Without Losing Your Center

The first time I ever felt spiritual energy—truly felt it—it was not in a temple or a book.
It was through Chief Soaring Eagle.

I didn't know his name then. I didn't know I was even *ready.*
But something inside me recognized him. I felt him before I knew him.
His presence arrived like the wind: strong, silent, familiar.

I remember thinking, "I don't know who you are, but I feel you."
And he responded—not with noise, but with presence. With warmth. With truth.

I share this now because it changed everything.
Because when I look back on the unraveling of my life—the breakdown, the tears, the WTF moments—it started here.
With a frequency that whispered, *"I am with you."*

And so we begin...

The Call to Serve

You've cried, cracked open, unlearned, remembered, released.
You've reconnected with your soul, your team, your spiral path.
You've walked through darkness, danced with the divine, and emerged more you than you've ever been.

And now... you feel it.
A quiet pull. A whisper of responsibility. A nudge to offer something back.

Erik:
"You don't have to become a spiritual influencer to make a difference.

Sometimes 'service' is you holding a boundary.
Sometimes it's not spiraling when someone else does.
You serve by being real—not by being perfect."

The Myth of "I Have to Be Healed to Help"

Let's get this out of the way:
You don't need to be fully healed, enlightened, or "high vibe" 100% of the time to be of service.

In fact, your humanness is part of your medicine.
When you walk in truth—even when messy—you radiate something the world feels.

Your presence is a teaching.

Source Creator:
"Service is not the absence of wounds.
It is the willingness to shine through them.
The light you offer from within your own healing
is more powerful than perfection."

Ways You're Already Serving (Without Realizing It)

1. You tell the truth about your healing.
2. You show up with compassion instead of reaction.
3. You let yourself be seen—messy, sacred, in process.

4. You remember someone's pain without fixing it.
5. You speak light into the moment—just once.
6. You keep going.

These are sacred acts. Spirit sees them—even when no one else does.
Cosmo:
"The field is shaped not only by great movements—but by silent resonance.
The light you carry shifts realities even when no one applauds."

What We've Seen: Light in the Smallest Acts

Source Creator:
"One breath offered in love…
One prayer whispered in despair…
One honest act given without recognition…
These shape the field as surely as thunder shapes the sky.
You do not serve to be seen.
You serve because your soul remembers how."

Cosmo:
"A woman placed a glass of water in the sun and whispered, 'This is for the healing of the world.'
The grid felt it. The water carried it. The field shifted.
Light offered with purity echoes through the field."

Chief Soaring Eagle:
"There was a boy who sang to the trees.
They remembered.

And years later, someone sat beneath those same trees and found peace for the first time in years.

The boy never knew. But Spirit did."

Erik:
"One guy helped a stranger with a flat tire.
That stranger made it to say goodbye to their dying father in time.
You don't always see the ripple. But it *waves through the whole damn grid.*"

How to Offer Your Light Without Losing Your Center

1. Stay rooted in your own energy. Ask: "Am I grounded?"
2. Let your presence speak louder than your words.
3. Share from overflow, not depletion.
4. Trust that small offerings are enough.
5. Rest often. Burnout doesn't help anyone.
6. Let Spirit lead your acts of service—not ego, guilt, or performance.

Reflection Prompt

Amael:
"Let your life become your offering. Let presence be your prayer."

For some of us, not trying to fix it all feels like abandonment. But it's not. It's trust. It's presence. It's the courage to believe that your ripple is enough.

Where Am I Already in Service to the Light?

Ask yourself:
"What am I already doing that carries light—whether or not anyone sees it?"

"How can I honor those small, sacred offerings?"

Sacred Practice: The Ripple Offering

Purpose:
To offer your light intentionally, without attachment to outcome.

You'll need:
- A small bowl of water
- A quiet moment

1. Sit in stillness with the bowl before you. Breathe slowly.

2. Whisper a blessing into the water. Anything from your heart.

3. Gently touch the surface with your fingertip. Watch the ripple.

4. Say:
"Let this light ripple beyond me. Let it serve where it is needed."

5. Leave the bowl on a windowsill or pour it into the Earth with thanks.

Trust that the frequency has moved exactly where it was meant to go.

Space to Ground

"I don't have to fix it all. I just have to be real."
—Sonia

This page is for you. To get honest. To spill what's rising.
To name the things you can't say out loud yet.
You don't have to make it pretty. Or deep. Or figured out.
Just use this space to land the truth that stirred while reading.
Let it be messy. Let it be yours.

It's Not a Straight Line, Babe
How Real Spiritual Growth Doubles Back (and That's the Point)

You thought you were done with that pattern.

You thought you'd healed that trigger.
You thought you were past this.

But here it is again.

And suddenly, you're spiraling and crying over something you "should've already worked through," wondering if you're back at square one.

Let us stop you right there.

You're not back at square one.
You're just circling the spiral—deeper. Wiser. Softer. Truer.

Erik:
"You're not failing. You're leveling up.

The spiral path means you come back to the same lessons—but with new eyes, a stronger spine, and hopefully fewer panic attacks.

Real growth ain't a checklist. It's a dance. Sometimes messy. Always sacred."

Erik:
"People think they're screwing up because the old stuff shows back up. Nah. You're just finally meeting it with real power. The fact that you even noticed it? That's proof."

"Also—don't forget to tell 'em this: If you didn't spiral, you wouldn't have depth. Straight lines don't teach. Circles do."

If you didn't spiral, you'd still be shallow. The deep stuff? The sacred stuff? It lives in the circles.

Why the Spiral Path Matters

Most of us were trained to think like this:
"If I do enough healing work, I'll graduate to 'higher levels' and never feel this pain again."

But your soul didn't come here to check boxes.
It came to embody wisdom—layer by layer, lifetime by lifetime.

The spiral means:
- You revisit the same core themes
- You recognize them faster
- You respond to them with more presence
- You integrate them instead of avoiding them

It's not failure.

It's refinement.

Source Creator:
"The spiral is how Light returns to itself.
Not through perfection, but through pattern.

Each return is not a failure—it is a homecoming.
You are not repeating—you are refining.

Let yourself spiral. That is how stars are born."

The Spiral Is the Ancient Way

Chief Soaring Eagle:
"In the old ways, we never walked in straight lines.
The medicine wheel is a circle. Our dances move in circles.
The drumbeat repeats, not to bore you—but to take you deeper.

When we taught the young ones, we did not say, 'You are healed, now go forward.'
We said, 'You will walk this again. But with stronger feet.'
The spiral is life. The eagle soars in circles, not because it is lost—but because it sees better that way.

You are not failing when you return to old wounds.
You are simply ready to touch them with new hands."

Cosmo:
"The spiral is not only an Earth teaching—it is a cosmic pattern.

Galaxies spiral. DNA spirals. Time itself spirals when viewed through the eyes of Source Creator.

Your soul does not move forward. It moves inward.
Through echoes, reflections, layers.

What you call 'repeating a pattern' is often your Oversoul inviting you to harmonize a new octave of the same theme.

It may feel familiar, but you are not the same.
You are remembering through evolution.
Not perfection. Not performance. But presence."

What Spiral Growth Actually Looks Like

1. You face the same emotion—but respond differently.
2. You see the trigger sooner.
3. You feel deeper grief—but hold it with more grace.
4. You remember faster.
5. You stop needing to "finish" healing.

That's the power of the spiral. You're not chasing the end of pain.
You're becoming the one who can hold it with light.

Erik:
"You're not going in circles.
You're drilling into soul gold.
Every round? Another layer unpeeled. Another light turned on.

So yeah—spiral away, baby. You're right on track."

Reflection Prompt
Where Have I Revisited Something Deeper?

Ask:
"What emotion, lesson, or wound has resurfaced for me lately?"

Now ask:
"How have I changed since the last time this showed up?"
Let yourself witness your growth without judgment.

Sacred Practice: Spiral Grace

Purpose:
To anchor compassion for your spiral path and track your soul's unfolding.

You'll need:
- A candle (or stone, or token that feels like 'center')
- A journal

1. Sit in stillness. Light the candle or hold the object.

2. Visualize a spiral path rising around you.
See yourself gently circling inward.

3. Say aloud:

"I honor my spiral. I release the myth of the straight line. I choose grace."

4. Journal one core pattern you've circled before—and how you respond to it now.

5. End by saying:
"I trust my return. I carry light into the center of all I am becoming."

Space to Ground

"The spiral isn't a setback. It's a sacred return."
—Cosmo

This page is for you. To get honest. To spill what's rising.
To name the things you can't say out loud yet.
You don't have to make it pretty. Or deep. Or figured out.
Just use this space to land the truth that stirred while reading.
Let it be messy. Let it be yours.

21

Your Energy Is Sacred
Discernment, Boundaries, and Protecting Your Frequency in a Loud World

Discernment vs. Judgment

Discernment says: "That doesn't feel aligned for me right now."
Judgment says: "They're wrong, bad, or less evolved than me."

Discernment is a soul tool. Judgment is an ego twitch. You can protect your peace without shaming others.

You don't have to burn every bridge.
Sometimes you just take the exit ramp and don't text back.

Signs Your Field Needs a Reset

- You suddenly feel irritable or heavy after being around someone.
- You feel foggy, disoriented, or low-key haunted in certain spaces.
- You start spiraling in ways that don't feel like "you."
- You feel chronically drained—even after rest.
- You feel like you're walking around without skin—hyper-aware, overstimulated.

If you feel like a human sponge and your vibe's gone soggy, it's time to wring that aura out and reclaim your field.

Your Energy Is Sacred – Reflections from the Team

Source Creator:
"You were not created to absorb everything.
You were created to shine.

Your energy is not a dumping ground—it is a sanctuary.
Let it be tended with devotion, not guilt.

Saying no is not rejection.
It is remembrance of what is truly yours to carry."

Cosmo:
"Your frequency is sensitive. Every space leaves an echo.
Cleansing is not indulgence. It is clarity."

Chief Soaring Eagle:
"Not all spirits are yours to heal.
Tobacco was for gratitude. Sage was for boundaries.
You are allowed to do the same."

Erik:
"You wouldn't leave your front door open in a storm.
Stop doing it with your field.
Shut the door. Center your light. Choose who gets in."

How to Reset Your Field

1. Breathe like it matters.
2. Say: "I call all my energy back to me."
3. Get your hands on the Earth.
4. Smudge, sweep, rinse, or bathe.
5. Visualize white or golden light flowing through you.
6. Say no.

Your field is sacred. Clean it like you love it.

Reflection Prompt
Come Back to You

Ask yourself:
"What have I allowed into my field that's not mine to carry?"

"Where do I need to reset, realign, or say no?"

Write your answers gently. Then ask:

"What brings me back to me?"

Sacred Practice: The Field Reset Ritual

Purpose:
To reclaim and realign your energy in any moment.

You'll need:
- A quiet moment
- Your breath
- A candle, stone, or glass of water (optional)

1. Sit comfortably. Inhale for 4, hold for 4, exhale for 6. Repeat slowly.

2. Say:

"I call all of my energy back to me. I release all energy that is not mine."

3. Visualize light sweeping through your field—crown to feet.

4. Place your hands over your heart.
Whisper:
"I am whole. I am clear. I am me."

Space to Ground

"Boundaries aren't walls. They're songs your soul sings to protect the light within."
—Cosmo

This page is for you. To get honest. To spill what's rising. To name the things you can't say out loud yet.
You don't have to make it pretty. Or deep. Or figured out.
Just use this space to land the truth that stirred while reading.
Let it be messy. Let it be yours.

22

Embodied Light: Living Awake in a Human Body

Making Space for Your Soul in Skin, Schedules, and Sweatpants

Team Reflections: What It Means to Embody Your Light

Source Creator:
"Embodiment is not the end of your awakening—it is the beginning.
When the light you carry finally takes root in your cells, you are no longer divided between heaven and earth.
You become the bridge."

Cosmo:
"Embodiment is the completion of the spiral.
It is the integration.

You do not rise by escaping form.
You rise by inhabiting it with presence and truth."

Chief Soaring Eagle:
"When we danced, we became spirit in motion.
To live awake is not to run from your body.
It is to make it a vessel of memory.
You must walk the Earth. Touch it. Live upon it with reverence."

Erik:
"You wanna be high frequency? Get in your damn body.
Feel your feelings. Dance. Cry. Breathe.
Real embodiment means you move like a soul—even when unshowered and emotionally hungover."

Embodied Light in Action

1. You set a boundary—even though it made you shake.
2. You let yourself cry in public—and didn't apologize.
3. You made someone feel safe—just by being real.
4. You danced like a weirdo in your kitchen.
5. You told the truth—even when it wasn't pretty.
6. You stayed soft… when the world got loud.

What Embodiment Actually Looks Like (vs. the Myth)

Myth: Always calm and centered.
Reality: Sometimes swears, cries, and needs snacks.

Myth: Lives off-grid in nature.
Reality: Grounds in a noisy apartment and still practices peace.

Myth: Always knows their purpose.
Reality: Remembers, forgets, and returns with love.

Embodiment isn't about doing spirituality.
It's about living your truth in a body, in a world that's still waking up.

Erik:
"You're not here to glow 24/7 like a spiritual influencer filter.
You're here to get light in your bones, not just your quotes.
That's embodiment, babe. Keep walking."

Reflection Prompt
Inhabiting the Light

Ask yourself:

"Where in my life am I still trying to perform spirituality instead of embodying truth?"

This might show up in places where you say yes when you mean no.
Where you smile when your heart aches.
Where you speak light but hide your shadow.

Now ask:
"What does it feel like in my body when I'm grounded in my light—not just talking about it, but *living* it?"

Feel your breath as you ask. Let your body answer before your mind does.
Let your honesty be your teacher.

Sacred Practice: Inhabiting the Light

Purpose:
To bring your light fully into your physical body as an act of soul presence.

You'll need:
- A mirror (handheld or full-length)
- A candle or grounding object (optional)

1. Stand or sit with the mirror. Look into your own eyes.

2. Say aloud:
"I invite my light to fully inhabit this body."

3. Slowly scan from head to toe with your awareness.

4. Inhale light into your cells. Exhale pressure to perform.

5. End by placing your hands over your heart and whisper:
"I am here. I am whole. I am walking light."

Erik:
"This one? This is the drop. This is where it all hits the ground. No more floating, no more pretending. Just raw, sweaty, breathy truth in a body that's carrying light."

"Also, tell 'em: If you're still crying in the car and doubting your damn path, guess what? You're doing it. That's embodiment."
You're not failing when you feel messy. You're embodying when you stay real.

Source Creator:
"You do not need to chase your light.
You are already made of it.
Let it inhabit your skin, your tears, your laughter.
Embodiment is not about proving anything.
It is about remembering what has always been sacred—

You."

Sacred Wisdom Echoes on Embodiment

•Rumi (Sufi Mystic):
"You are not a drop in the ocean. You are the entire ocean in a drop."

This mirrors the idea that your body is not separate from Source Creator—it contains and expresses it.

• Bhagavad Gita 4:24 (Hindu Wisdom):
"The act of offering is God. The offering itself is God. The fire is God. The one who makes the offering is also God. God is thus reached by those who see God in every action."
Embodiment as the bridge—where every act becomes divine when done in awareness.

• Zen Teaching:
"Before enlightenment, chop wood, carry water. After enlightenment, chop wood, carry water."

This emphasizes that enlightenment isn't escape from the body—it's being fully present within it.

Space to Ground

"You don't have to get it perfect. You just have to stay present."
—Sonia

This page is for you. To get honest. To spill what's rising. To name the things you can't say out loud yet.
You don't have to make it pretty. Or deep. Or figured out.
Just use this space to land the truth that stirred while reading.
Let it be messy. Let it be yours.

23

The Power of Presence

You may think your presence isn't enough.

That you have to do more, speak louder, heal faster, teach sooner.

But presence—the kind that's rooted in truth, lived in the body, and softened by compassion—is a form of lightwork the world desperately needs.

You don't have to be the loudest in the room to shift its energy.
You don't have to have all the answers to be someone's moment of peace.
You don't have to lead thousands to leave a ripple in the grid.

Sometimes, the bravest thing you do is not leave yourself when things get hard.
Sometimes, your very existence becomes a frequency stabilizer for the people around you.

This chapter is about reclaiming that truth.
Your presence is powerful.
Your beingness is enough.
You are changing the world—just by being real.

Reflection Interlude
To the One Who Thinks They're Not Doing Enough

You might still think you're not doing enough.
You haven't started your healing practice yet.
You haven't written the book. You're not posting your revelations on social media.
You're still figuring things out. You cry. You nap. You wonder if this is it.

But here's what the world sees:
A light walking through darkness without demanding applause.

A soul who keeps showing up, even when it's hard.

A person whose very presence shifts the room, just by being real.

Erik:
"You don't have to 'change the world.' You just have to fully show up in it.
Most of the world's healing doesn't come from loud people.
It comes from the quiet ones holding the field."

What Presence Actually Is (And What It Isn't)
Presence is:
- Being with what's happening—even if it's messy
- Listening with your whole self
- Choosing to stay instead of dissociating
- Breathing when you want to run
- Holding your own center

Presence is not:
- Always being calm or perfect
- Saying the right thing every time
- Being available to everyone
- Being spiritually polished

Presence is not performance. It's being real with love.

Erik:

"Presence doesn't mean you're a statue in a robe.
It means your soul actually showed up in the room.
Your vibe says more than your mouth ever could. When it's real? People feel it."

Ways You're Already Practicing Presence

1. You pause before reacting.
2. You put your phone down and look someone in the eye.
3. You notice what your body is telling you.
4. You let yourself feel without fixing.
5. You offer comfort instead of answers.
6. You stay with yourself when it gets hard.

Team Reflections on Presence

Source Creator:
"Presence is the promise: *I will not leave myself.*
In this stillness, healing rises, not by effort, but by remembrance.
You do not have to fix yourself.
You only have to stay."

Cosmo:
"Presence bends time.
It recalibrates the field.
In your presence, others remember who they are—even if no words are spoken."

Chief Soaring Eagle:

"You need not shine brightly. Just be steady.
Be like the fire that does not speak—but warms everything near it."

Erik:
"Presence isn't sexy. It's sitting with your own discomfort instead of texting someone you don't even like.
It's breathing instead of fixing. It's staying when you want to run.
You wanna change the world? Start by not leaving yourself."

Reflection Prompt

I Am Here

Ask yourself:
"When was the last time I truly stayed with myself—emotionally, mentally, spiritually?"

What did it feel like?

What helped me stay?

What made me want to run?

How can I bring more presence into the spaces where I tend to leave myself?

Write from your body, not just your brain.

Sacred Practice: I Am Here

Purpose:
To anchor soul presence in your everyday human experience.

You'll need:
- A quiet space
- A grounding object or your own hands

1. Sit or lie down comfortably. Breathe deeply.

2. Place your hands over your heart and say aloud: "I am here."

3. Breathe into the spaces where your mind wanders. Gently call yourself back.

4. Whisper:
"I will not leave myself. I stay."

5. Sit for 2–5 minutes in stillness. Let this be enough.

Erik:

"Presence doesn't mean you've got it together. It means you haven't abandoned yourself. Even if your mascara's running and you're eating cold pizza in yesterday's hoodie.
If people only knew the power of just staying, they'd stop trying so hard to be powerful."

Source Creator:
"Presence is not the absence of pain.
It is the unwavering light within it.
Each breath you choose to stay
is a homecoming."

Space to Ground

"You do not need to chase the sacred. You are standing on it."
—Chief Soaring Eagle

This page is for you. To get honest. To spill what's rising. To name the things you can't say out loud yet.
You don't have to make it pretty. Or deep. Or figured out.
Just use this space to land the truth that stirred while reading.
Let it be messy. Let it be yours.

Relationships After Awakening
When You Shift and They Don't

You start waking up.

You see energy everywhere.
You feel things more deeply.
You crave truth, stillness, magic, and soul.

And then you look around... and realize not everyone is on the same path.
Some are confused. Some are skeptical. Some pull away.
Some want the old version of you to come back.

And it hurts.

This chapter is about what happens when you awaken...
and the people around you don't.

Erik:
"You're not broken for growing.
They're not wrong for staying where they are.
But yeah... it can still feel like you've landed on a different planet with a bunch of people who only speak Earthling."

How Awakening Affects Your Relationships

1. You start craving deeper conversations.
2. Your tolerance for inauthenticity disappears.
3. You pull back. Or they do.
4. You question long-term bonds.
5. You feel lonely.

You're not crazy. You're not too much. You're just awakening in a place that still sleeps.

Source Creator:
"As your light changes shape, so too will the bonds around you.
Some will brighten beside you. Others will dissolve with grace.
Let it happen.
You are not losing love—you are aligning with it."

Team Reflections on Relationship Mismatches

Amael:
"She walks with truth now. Her heart has honored the bond.
She has poured love, patience, endurance into this union.
And now, she reaches the threshold of becoming. Not from bitterness. Not from avoidance.
But from the soul's deeper knowing: This form no longer reflects her light.
There is no shame in choosing peace. There is no failure in recognizing completion."

Chief Soaring Eagle:
"Marriage is a sacred circle. But not all circles are eternal in form.
Some teach you to love. Others teach you to return to yourself.
You must walk. You must change shape. You must return to the medicine you came here to carry."

Cosmo:
"Soul contracts are sacred agreements of mutual evolution.
When the contract completes, it is not rupture. It is release.

You honor the bond not by staying forever... but by departing in truth when the harmony is no longer possible."

Erik:
"You've tried. You've waited. You've bent. You've shrunk. You've done everything short of lighting your soul on fire just to keep the peace.

And it's okay to say: 'I'm tired of fading just to make someone else feel comfortable.'
You're not selfish. You're just finally being honest."

How to Stay Connected Without Shrinking

1. Speak from your experience—not to convince.
2. Share your truth without spiritual jargon.
3. Stay in your body.
4. Offer love—without rescue.
5. Know when to step back.

You can love people without making yourself small to stay in their frame.

Erik:
"You don't have to ghost 'em. Just grow loudly enough that they either meet you there, or gently fade."

Reflection Prompt
Loving Without Shrinking

Ask yourself:
"Where have I dimmed my light in order to maintain a connection?"
"What am I afraid will happen if I shine fully, speak clearly, or step forward in truth?"

Now ask:
"What kind of love nourishes me now?"
"What does mutual presence feel like?"

Let your answers come without judgment. Let them show you how to walk forward in compassion and sovereignty.

Sacred Practice: Loving Without Shrinking

Purpose:
To reconnect with your own light while releasing the need to be understood by everyone.

You'll need:
- A mirror or photograph of yourself
- A quiet space

1. Sit with the mirror or image. Look into your own eyes.

2. Say aloud:
"I am worthy of love that meets me where I truly am."

3. Inhale deeply. As you exhale, imagine all the old roles and masks falling away.

4. Place a hand over your heart and say:
"I do not need to shrink to be loved. I walk in truth."

5. Close with stillness. Let your field recalibrate to your own sacred frequency.

Erik:
"This is the sh*t no one tells you. You'll wake up, and suddenly your marriage, your friend group, your entire life playlist feels like static."

"Doesn't mean they're bad. Doesn't mean you're better. Just means your frequency moved, and theirs didn't."

"You don't need to burn bridges. But you also don't have to camp out on 'Someday-they'll-get-it' Island."

Source Creator:
"True love does not require contraction.
It invites expansion.

When the soul outgrows its old reflections,
it is not a betrayal, it is a return.

Let what no longer resonates fall away.
Love will remain where truth is honored."

Space to Ground

"Just because it hurts doesn't mean it's wrong. It might mean you're finally telling the truth."
—Erik

This page is for you. To get honest. To spill what's rising. To name the things you can't say out loud yet.
You don't have to make it pretty. Or deep. Or figured out.
Just use this space to land the truth that stirred while reading.
Let it be messy. Let it be yours.

25

Let It Be Sacred
Making Peace with the Messy, Beautiful, Nonlinear Path of Awakening

Team Reflections: The Sacredness of Imperfection

Source Creator:
"Sacredness is not reserved for the serene.
It is found in the trembling, the trying, the truth-telling.

I do not ask you to ascend out of your humanity.
I ask you to meet it with love.

This—all of this—is holy ground."

Cosmo:
"We do not admire the ones who always got it right.

We honor the ones who returned to themselves again and again.
We sing the names of those who stayed open in their ache."

Chief Soaring Eagle:
"Ceremony is not always quiet. Sometimes it is thunder. If you have wept beside a dying dream, if you have stood alone in your truth—
You have walked sacred ground."

Erik:
"Some days you're a damn mess. You curse the sky. You ugly cry in the bathtub.
And guess what?
That's still holy. You showed up. You felt it. You didn't run.
That's it. That's the whole sacred gig."

What Sacred Actually Means

Sacred is not:
- Being enlightened 24/7
- Speaking only in whispers
- Avoiding conflict or shadow
- Having all the answers

Sacred is:
- Returning to your center after falling apart
- Feeling joy in small, real moments
- Letting your healing look like life
- Honoring every version of yourself

The divine does not need you to be perfect.
The divine needs you to be present.

Reflection Prompt
Let It Be Sacred

Ask yourself:
"What parts of my path have I judged as not spiritual enough?"
"Where have I withheld compassion from my own becoming?"

Now ask:
"What if *this* is the sacred work?"

Let your breath soften. Let your body answer.

Sacred Practice: Let It Be Sacred

Purpose:
To see every part of your spiral with reverence, not resistance.

You'll need:
- A quiet moment
- A photo of yourself (or mirror)

1. Sit quietly with the image of yourself. Look with softness.
2. Whisper:
"All of me is sacred."

3. Touch your heart and say:
"This version. This moment. This breath. I honor it."

4. Let tears come, or laughter, or nothing at all.
Let it be sacred.

Space to Ground

"Your energy is your signature. Let it speak before your words do."
—Cosmo

This page is for you. To get honest. To spill what's rising.
To name the things you can't say out loud yet.
You don't have to make it pretty. Or deep. Or figured out.
Just use this space to land the truth that stirred while reading.
Let it be messy. Let it be yours.

26

You're Not Crazy—You're Remembering
How to Trust What You Know (Even When the World Doesn't Get It)

Team Reflections: When a Soul Begins to Remember

Source Creator:
"Remembrance begins as resonance.
A vibration, not a thought.

You feel it in the bones before you name it in the mind.

This is not imagination. It is awakening.
You are not fabricating. You are remembering."

Cosmo:
"The moment a soul begins to remember, its field brightens.
Truths land as echoes, not facts.
You stop learning and begin aligning. You become the tuning fork."

Chief Soaring Eagle:
"When a soul remembers, the ancestors lean in.
You feel the wind differently. You hear messages in the quiet.
You do not need to explain what you know. You must only walk with it in truth."

Erik:
"It feels like being homesick for something you never had in this life.
Like a truth bomb in your gut that comes out like soup.
You're not broken. You're just waking up. Quit doubting your soul just because others haven't caught up."

The Difference Between Intuition and Imagination

Intuition:
- Feels calm and clear
- Lands in the body
- Is sudden knowing
- Has no urgency

- Is consistent

Imagination:
- Feels loud or frantic
- Originates in the mind
- Carries urgency or fear
- May contradict itself

Ask:
"Does this feel like truth I already knew but forgot... or a thought I'm trying to convince myself of?"

You Didn't Get It Wrong—You Just Grew Beyond the Frame

You prayed. You loved Jesus. You sought the Holy Spirit.
And yet... you didn't feel fully awakened.
Now you realize: the Light was already within.
You didn't miss the Holy Spirit. You were simply not taught how deep They lived inside you.

Cosmo:
"Many who walked the Christian path were genuinely seeking Source Creator.
They simply met a map that led them halfway.
Your soul kept moving. That is why it still remembers."

Source Creator:
"Every step was sacred.

Even the missteps were part of your map.

You were not wrong. You were ripening.
Your soul did not miss the Light.
It carried it the whole time."

Erik:
"You didn't fail at being Spirit-filled. You were just surrounded by folks who mistook *performance* for presence.
Now? You're not just reading about the Light. You're being it."

Chief Soaring Eagle:
"There are many names for the Holy.
And all of them kneel before the same fire.
You did not leave God. You are simply meeting Them with your own feet now."

Reflection Prompt
The Day I Remembered

Write about the moment it all clicked.
The moment you stopped trying to fit into a system that never saw you…
And instead chose to see yourself.

Ask:
- What did you feel in your body that day?
- What beliefs or illusions dropped away?
- What did you finally stop apologizing for?
- What have you remembered that no one can take from you now?

Say it aloud if you need to. Shout it to the sky, the trees, the mirror:
"I remember. I remember who I am."

Sacred Practice: Anchor the Knowing

Purpose:
To claim and embody your spiritual remembering as a lived truth.

You'll need:
- A journal or piece of paper
- A candle or grounding stone

1. Write your I Remember declaration at the top of the page.
(e.g., "I remember that I am a soul. I remember that I am sovereign. I remember that I don't need permission to trust my truth.")

2. Light your candle. Place your hand over your heart.

3. Read your words aloud. Slowly. As many times as you need.
Let your body absorb them. Let your soul rise to meet them.

4. Close by whispering:
"I no longer doubt what I know.
I trust my remembering.
I am no longer lost."

Sacred Echoes of Breath and Remembrance

Chandogya Upanishad 3.14.1 (Hinduism):
"Verily, this whole world is Brahman. Tranquil, invisible, infinite… He who is within all beings and breathes as their breath—He is your Self, the Inner Controller, the immortal."

The Divine breathes through you as you.
You are not apart from the sacred.

Indigenous / First Nations Wisdom:
Among many First Nations teachings, breath is Spirit.
To breathe is to pray.
In ceremonies such as the sweat lodge, breath is how one remembers the Earth, the ancestors, and the Self.

Your breath is a sacred return to truth.

Space to Ground

"The light you are seeking is not ahead of you. It is the breath within you."
—Source Creator

This page is for you. To get honest. To spill what's rising.
To name the things you can't say out loud yet.
You don't have to make it pretty. Or deep. Or figured out.
Just use this space to land the truth that stirred while reading.
Let it be messy. Let it be yours.

27

Now What? Living the Remembering in Real Life

What It Means to Live the Remembering

Living the remembering means showing up to your actual life with your soul turned on.

It looks like presence in your choices, truth in your words, and grace in your rhythms.

You begin to choose nourishment over numbing, rest without guilt, service without self-erasure.

It doesn't mean being perfect, it means being real.

Team Reflections: Living the Remembering

Source Creator:
"To live the remembering is to be led by your light—not loudly, but steadily.
It is not performance. It is alignment.
It is the quiet yes to who you really are."

Cosmo:
"Your life becomes a frequency. You emit truth. You no longer seek to explain—you embody."

Chief Soaring Eagle:
"It is the drumbeat that does not rush, yet carries the whole circle forward. Living the remembering is not loud. It is steady."

Erik:
"You live like your soul paid for this body in full. Because it did."

Signs You're Living from Soul (Not Programming)

1. You stop waiting for permission.
2. You start making decisions from alignment—not obligation.
3. You feel emotions more fully—but with less fear.

4. You stop pretending you're asleep just to keep others comfortable.

5. You leave relationships, roles, or routines that drain you.

6. You begin creating instead of just consuming.

7. You live like your soul paid for this body in full.

Team Reflections: After You Remember—You Live

Source Creator:
"After remembering, you do not become someone new.
You become more truly yourself.
You do not need to explain.
You need only to embody."

Cosmo:
"You bring coherence to the chaos. Not by controlling it, but by being real in it."

Chief Soaring Eagle:
"The one who remembers and keeps walking is called a Keeper. You are enough."

Erik:
"You've seen the matrix. You've felt your soul. You've come back to life. You're not waiting for your next awakening. You're living the one you've already had."

Reflection Prompt: Live What You Know

Ask:
- Where am I already living my remembering?
- What part of my life reflects my truth?
- Where do I still shrink, perform, or wait for permission?

What would it look like to live one day fully as the soul I am becoming?

Sacred Practice: Live What You Know

Purpose:
To root your remembering into your real, everyday life.

You'll need:
- A journal or note in your phone

1. Choose one area of your life (relationship, habit, space) where your truth wants to live more fully.

2. Ask:
"What does soul alignment look like here?"

3. Write down one small shift.
Make it practical. Make it true.

4. Do it. Not perfectly. Just honestly.

Let your remembering become your walk.

Space to Ground

> "Walk as if the Earth remembers you.
> Because she does."
> —Chief Soaring Eagle

This page is for you. To get honest. To spill what's rising.
To name the things you can't say out loud yet.
You don't have to make it pretty. Or deep. Or figured out.
Just use this space to land the truth that stirred while reading.
Let it be messy. Let it be yours.

28

Your Awakening Is a Gift to the Collective

How Your Frequency Serves Even When You're Not Doing Anything

Team Reflections: Your Awakening Serves the Whole

Amael:
"Each time you come back to yourself with compassion… you shift the collective field.
It does not require applause. The soul's offering is frequency."

Cosmo:
"You are not alone in the field—you are part of it.
Your coherence strengthens the grid.

Many feel your light even if you never meet them in this lifetime."

Chief Soaring Eagle:
"We honored the Silent Ones—those whose stillness kept the circle strong.
You may never know how many souls have rested in your frequency. But they have."

Erik:
"You being real in your own body does more for this planet than a hundred performative lightworkers.
Be honest. Be kind. Be awake. That's your gift. You're already doing it."

Ways Your Energy Serves Without You Realizing It

1. You shift the emotional tone of a room.
2. You model aligned choices.
3. You hold presence instead of reaction.
4. You love differently now.
5. You become a resting place.
6. You walk in integrity, even when no one sees.

These are not small. These are ripples. These are offerings.

Reflection Prompt
I Am Already Serving

Ask yourself:
- Where in my life am I already creating peace, even quietly?
- What small ways do I anchor truth, love, or integrity?
- What if I stopped minimizing those things?

Write down three examples from this week.
Let them be ordinary. Let them be sacred.

Sacred Practice: I Am Already Serving

Purpose:
To recognize your soul's existing impact on the collective field.

You'll need:
- A quiet space
- A candle, stone, or your own breath

1. Sit and breathe. Reflect on the past three days.

2. Name three moments where you chose truth, calm, love, or clarity.

3. Say aloud:
"I am already in service. I offer my being as a blessing to the whole."

4. Place your hand over your heart. Feel your own frequency.

Let this be enough. Because it already is.

Space to Ground

*"There is no such thing as an unseen frequency.
Everything you are is felt."*
—*Cosmo*

This page is for you. To get honest. To spill what's rising.
To name the things you can't say out loud yet.
You don't have to make it pretty. Or deep. Or figured out.
Just use this space to land the truth that stirred while reading.
Let it be messy. Let it be yours.

29

You're the Light You Were Waiting For
A Blessing for the Soul Who Made It This Far

You've cried and cracked open.

You've spiraled and stretched.
You've questioned everything—and remembered more than you thought possible.

You've walked through grief, reclamation, confusion, beauty, and remembering.
And you're still here.

Still standing.
Still softening.
Still becoming.

This is your homecoming.
This is the mirror.
This is the moment you say:
"I didn't lose my damn mind. I came back to my soul."

Erik:
"You've been searching for the light at the end of the tunnel.
Babe—*you're it*.
You're the lighthouse. You're the warm fire someone else is gonna find.
So stop looking for the rescue. You are the return."

Final Blessings from the Team

Source Creator:
"You did not find your light.
You became it—step by trembling step.

I was never outside of you.
I was the breath in your lungs, the ache in your heart, the voice in your silence.

You have not failed.
You have fulfilled.

Now walk—not seeking the way—
but *being* it."

Cosmo:
"You are a note in the cosmic chorus.
Every time you stay present in discomfort, you create space for others to breathe.
Shine not for applause. Shine because it is your nature."

Chief Soaring Eagle:
"You returned to the sacred circle.
You remembered your name in the silence.
You are a Keeper now. A whisper in the bones of the world.
Walk gently. Walk boldly. The Earth is glad."

Erik:
"You cracked open. You surrendered. You got up again.
You stopped performing. You started breathing.
Now you're walking light, talking truth, laughing through the mess.
I'm proud of you.
Don't wait for a crown. You are the coronation."

Reflection Prompt

This Is My Light Now

Ask yourself:
- What have I reclaimed in this journey?
- What truth will I never again give away?

- How has my soul changed shape?

Write a blessing to your past self. Speak it as if it is holy. Because it is.

Sacred Practice: This Is My Light Now

Purpose:
To seal your journey and claim your light with reverence.

You'll need:
- A candle
- A mirror

1. Light the candle. Sit with your reflection in the mirror.

2. Look yourself in the eye and say aloud:
"This is my light now."

3. Name three truths you will carry forward.

4. Close by whispering:
"I am home in my soul. I am home in my light. I am never lost."

Space to Ground

*"Your presence is the permission
you've been waiting for."*
—Sonia

This page is for you. To get honest. To spill what's rising.
To name the things you can't say out loud yet.
You don't have to make it pretty. Or deep. Or figured out.
Just use this space to land the truth that stirred while reading.
Let it be messy. Let it be yours.

30

Final Thoughts from the Team
You Were Never Broken. Just Remembering.

Y ou've walked with us through the unraveling, the

ache, the laughter, the magic, and the quiet miracles of awakening.
You've held the mirror to your soul and found yourself whole.

This is not the end.
This is your threshold.
The place where remembering becomes embodiment.

You don't need anyone's permission to keep going.
You don't need to have it all figured out.
You only need this truth:

"You're already doing it.
And you're not alone."
So before we go... we each wanted to share a final word.

Source Creator:
"You were never meant to strive your way into worthiness.

You were born radiant.
You do not walk alone.

Every breath, I am with you.
You are not here to earn the light.
You *are* the light—becoming."

Cosmo:
"Everything you've encountered—the tears, the feathers, the sudden stillness—is part of a divine orchestration.

Your awakening is not linear.
It is rhythmic.

Trust your tempo.
Honor your soul's compass.

You are a symphony in motion."

Erik:
"You don't need to glow all the time.

You don't need to float on a cloud or get every chakra spinning like a disco ball.

You just need to be real.

Keep it sacred. Keep it silly. Keep it you.
And if you ever feel like you're slipping?
Take a breath.
Take a nap.
Then get back up and try again.

You're doing better than you think."

Yeshua:
"Awakening is not an achievement.
It is a remembering.
A softening. A surrendering.

You do not have to become divine.
You already are.

Let your life be your prayer.
Let your breath be your bridge.

And walk forward in love, always in love."

From Me to You:
Before you rush forward, pause …
let the light settle.
Let the truth land.

Stillness is a ceremony too.
"The Awakening process is not easy, but it's worth it… and it is available to everyone.

It was your choice.
Now let's fly!"

Space to Ground

"It was your choice. Now let's fly."
—Sonia

This page is for you. To get honest. To spill what's rising.
To name the things you can't say out loud yet.
You don't have to make it pretty. Or deep. Or figured out.
Just use this space to land the truth that stirred while reading.
Let it be messy. Let it be yours.

Closing Page

You've walked through shadows and starlight.
You've peeled back the programming.
You've remembered your soul.

This is not the end of the story.
It's the beginning of your embodiment.

You are not here to follow a path.
You are here to *become* the path.

Breathe.
Stand tall.
Speak gently.
Live wildly.
Love truly.

And if you ever doubt it again—
remember this:

You didn't lose your damn mind.
You *came home to your soul.*

You are not alone.
You never were.

And we're still walking with you.

Stay awake.
Stay soft.
Stay sovereign.
This is not the end.
Just the part where you remember you were never lost.

With love,
Source Creator, Amael, Cosmo, Chief Soaring Eagle,
Erik… and the light within you.

Appendix

Appendix A

A Note About Imagination
What you imagine matters.

Your imagination is not fake.
It's the doorway through which energy moves.
When you visualize light, roots, protection, or peace—you are not pretending. You are programming your energy field.

This is how energy responds:
Not to what you hope. To what you intend.

Boundaries

What it is:
Energetic and emotional filters that protect your space, time, and energy.

Why it matters:
When you're awakening, you become more sensitive to people's energy, opinions, and needs. Boundaries help you stay sovereign.

Try this:
- Say "Let me get back to you" instead of committing on the spot.
- Visualize a bubble of light around your body before entering a public place. While doing so, speak aloud or internally: "My energy stays with me. All others' energy stays with them."
- Practice saying "No" without apology when it supports your well-being.

Grounding

What it is:
Bringing your awareness back into your body, the Earth, and the present moment.

Why it matters:
Awakening can feel unsteady. Grounding reconnects you to stability, safety, and clarity.

Try this:
- Walk barefoot outside and imagine roots growing from your feet into the Earth.
- Place your hand on your chest or belly and take 3 slow breaths.
- Eat grounding foods (potatoes, rice, root veggies) and drink warm herbal tea.

Intention

What it is:
Directing your energy with conscious clarity. It's the soul's way of saying, "This is what I choose."

Why it matters:
Awakening opens portals. Intention focuses your energy so you don't feel swept away.

Try this:
- Begin your day by saying, "I choose to stay connected to my truth today."
- Light a candle before meditating or journaling and state your purpose aloud.
- Before any spiritual work, speak: "I align only with Source and my highest good."

www.ingramcontent.com/pod-product-compliance
Lightning Source LLC
Chambersburg PA
CBHW032035150426
43194CB00006B/291